CHINA'S URBAN CHRISTIANS

Studies in Chinese Christianity

G. Wright Doyle and Carol Lee Hamrin,

Series Editors

A Project of the Global China Center

www.globalchinacenter.org

China's Urban Christians

A Light That Cannot Be Hidden

BRENT FULTON

PICKWICK *Publications* · Eugene, Oregon

CHINA'S URBAN CHRISTIANS
A Light That Cannot Be Hidden

Pickwick Publications
An Imprint of Wipf and Stock Publishers
199 W. 8th Ave., Suite 3
Eugene, OR 97401

www.wipfandstock.com

ISBN 13: 978-1-62564-719-1

Cataloguing-in-Publication Data

Fulton, Brent

China's urban Christians : a light that cannot be hidden / Brent Fulton.

x + 146 p. ; 23 cm. Includes bibliographical references and index.

ISBN 13: 978-1-62564-719-1

1. China—Church history. 2. China—Religion. 3. Christianity—China. I. Title. II. Series.

BR1296 F85 2015

Manufactured in the U.S.A.   11/11/2015

Cover photograph by Gaylan Yeung.

For Jasmine

Contents

Acknowledgments

Special thanks to the following individuals, without whose encouragement and gracious assistance this book would not have been possible:

Carol Lee Hamrin and Wright Doyle of Global China Center for suggesting the project, offering helpful guidance throughout the process, and providing critical comments on earlier drafts;

My colleague, Emerald Lam, for her assistance in setting up interviews;

Narci Herr of ChinaSource for her careful copy editing of the finished manuscript;

The many Christians in China and those serving among them, most of whom cannot be mentioned by name, who shared their stories and insights;

Joann Pittman of ChinaSource, who provided valuable documentary material through the Chinese Church Voices project;

My parents, John and Mary Jo Fulton, for their steadfast support throughout the years of my China-related study and research;

My loving wife, Jasmine, to whom this book is dedicated, for her inspiration, faithful encouragement, and companionship on our shared journey;

Above all, to the Chief Cornerstone, whose proclamation, "I will build My Church," continues to be fulfilled in the lives of tens of millions of His followers in cities across China.

1

Introduction

*"You are the light of the world. A city that is set
on a hill cannot be hidden."*[1]

URBANIZATION IS INDELIBLY REDRAWING the landscape of China, geographically, as well as socially. A prominent feature of China's meteoric rise
in this century, the unprecedented growth of its cities has in many ways
been the driving force behind China's extraordinary economic growth and
development. New manufacturing centers springing up in eastern and
southern China became magnets for foreign investment in the nation's
cities, both old and new, fueling advances in technology, education, and
infrastructure development. Those same cities drew hundreds of thousands
of peasants into this whirlwind of economic activity, with migrant workers
making possible China's industrial boom and the massive building projects
that have been essential to the nation's rise.

Another phenomenon has also emerged, somewhat unexpectedly, as
a prominent feature of China's rise. The growth of religion, in particular
Christianity, has caught the attention of journalists and scholars alike as
they have explored the various facets of China's rapidly changing society.
From *Jesus in Beijing* by former *Time* magazine Beijing bureau chief David Aikman[2] to Gerda Wielander's *Christian Values in Communist China*[3]

1. Matthew 5:14.
2. Aikman, *Jesus in Beijing.*
3. Wielander, *Christian Values.*

a decade later, observers have endeavored to interpret the surprising re-emergence of Christianity following decades of harsh persecution and to anticipate how this growing movement might affect China's future. Both Lian Xi[4] and Daniel Bays[5] have put today's church growth into historical context, showing the continuities between Christian life in the current era and the development of the church in China before 1949. Liao Yiwu's vivid retelling of the stories of individual believers provides insights into how the church withstood formidable obstacles to become a vibrant social force in many parts of China.[6] Carol Hamrin and Jason Kindopp,[7] and more recently Timothy Conkling,[8] have examined how Christians face repression by China's authoritarian regime. In their investigation into China's "religious awakening," Rodney Stark and Wang Xiuhu used statistical analysis to substantiate claims of Christianity's rapid growth—from just over one million Protestants and 3.2 million Catholics in 1950 to slightly over 60 million Christians by 2007—and to show how this growth is taking place among both rural peasants and the well-educated in China (albeit for different reasons).[9]

This book is an attempt to bring together these two facets of China's rise—urbanization and the emergence of a significant and growing Christian community. Although contemporary studies of Christianity in China have acknowledged the role of urbanization as a component of the overall social landscape, the specific implications of urbanization for the church and, conversely, of Christianity for the city, have received comparatively little attention. The purpose of this book is to explore how the church in China perceives the challenges posed by its new urban context and to examine its proposed means of responding to these challenges. "Church" here is used in the broad sense to refer to the community of Christians in China. The specific focus will be on Protestant Christianity, although parallels to much of what is taking place in urban Protestant communities may also be found among Catholic believers, in both the registered church under the Catholic Patriotic Association and in the unregistered churches.

---

4. Xi, *Redeemed by Fire*.

5. Bays, *A New History of Christianity in China*.

6. Liao, *God is Red*.

7. Hamrin and Kindopp, *God and Caesar in China*.

8. Conkling, *Mobilized Merchants–Patriotic Martyrs*.

9. Stark and Wang, *A Star in the East*.

AN INCOMPLETE NARRATIVE

In contrast to much contemporary literature on Christianity in China, the present study does not see the church's current challenges as being primarily political in nature. Much of this literature positions the church as one of many unofficial social groupings that stand outside the direct reach of—and sometimes in opposition to—the authoritarian party-state. Since the party-state is officially atheistic, religious groups are seen as posing a particular threat to the regime. Their allegiance to a power other than that of the regime threatens the party-state's authoritarian grip on society; thus religious believers have been suspect in the eyes of China's leaders and have historically been objects of repression.[10] This "David vs. Goliath" view of the church-state relationship has given rise to a prevailing "persecution" narrative, which paints a picture of a struggling church victimized by an all-powerful state bent on its demise.[11]

As will be seen in chapter eight, many of the assumptions underlying this narrative remain valid. The boundaries of acceptable Christian activity are still set by the regime and are subject to change. In recent decades, however, these boundaries have loosened considerably. In this environment the prevailing "persecution" narrative does not begin to tell the whole story, nor does it do justice to the intricate and multi-faceted reality of most Christians in China today. While intense persecution was the norm during the Cultural Revolution, the situation for the church during the past thirty years has been less clear-cut and much more complex as the regime's attention has moved from ideological purity to economic development.

The central issue for China's Christians has shifted from freedom of belief to freedom of association.[12] Those who choose to organize in ways that are perceived as threatening to the regime risk reprisal. Included among these are Christians who, whether through direct confrontation or through working creatively within the system, seek political change that will allow the church to fulfill what they see as its proper role in Chinese society. Other Christians in China are active in building civil society institutions, with many playing a leading role in China's nascent NGO sector.[13]

---

10. "Cracks in the atheist edifice."
11. Fulton, "In Their Own Words," 99–100.
12. Carol Lee Hamrin, email message to author, June 17, 2015.
13. "Cracks in the Atheist Edifice."

CHALLENGES OF A CHANGING URBAN ENVIRONMENT

For most of China's Christians, however, political and social change are not the priority. The challenges they face lie much closer to home, as China's Christians seek to define how the church should function in its new urban environment. Raising up a new generation of qualified leadership, managing church affairs, maintaining the integrity of the faith amidst an onslaught of secularizing forces, meeting the practical needs of believers, and articulating the church's mission in a manner relevant to its urban context are among the issues that are top-of-mind for Christians in China today.

The exploration of this agenda suggests the following questions:

- How have church structures changed as the church has moved from a primarily rural to an urban setting?
- What kind of church leadership is emerging?
- Given the church's urban setting, how has the church's mission changed in the minds of its leaders?
- How do China's Christians see the church relating to China's urban society?
- How might Christians in China be expected to engage with the global Christian community?

The exploration begins by examining the backdrop of widespread demographic, social, and cultural change against which the challenges facing China's Christians are to be viewed, thus laying the groundwork for addressing these challenges in detail in later chapters. Chapter three shows how the church's shift is both geographical and generational; together these changes have resulted in a transformation of the church that encompasses its leadership, structure, physical location, and position in society. Chapter four examines how the shifts explored earlier have created a new environment of comparative openness in which the greatest threats facing the church are not political but social and cultural, posing new challenges to the individual and community life of Christians in China. Chapter five looks at how Christians perceive, and seek to respond to, widely recognized social problems that have accompanied decades of rapid change absent a shared moral and ethical system. Amidst this "crisis of faith," many among China's Christians see an imperative for social engagement, which takes multiple forms in China's urban context.

As China's opening has resulted in greater integration with the international community, Chinese believers are beginning to explore their role in the global community of faith, particularly in the task of world evangelization. Chapter six surveys the motivations and activities surrounding this conscious move outward. Chapter seven takes a look at both the new opportunities for, and obstacles to, unity within the church that are brought about by increased social openness and a new generation of leaders who see as a priority their ability to work together. Standing against this impetus for unity are an underlying culture of mistrust and the prospect of the church dividing along denominational or theological lines. The book concludes by revisiting the thesis that the most formidable challenges facing Christians in China have more to do with the church's changing social and cultural environment than they do with direct political pressure.

LISTENING TO THE CHINESE CHURCH

Although a wide variety of academic and popular sources are consulted in order to fill out this picture of China's urban church, throughout the book there is a conscious attempt to hear from the church itself and to allow individual Christians in China to tell their story. Much of this documentary material has come through dozens of conversations and interviews with Chinese Christians. In addition, *Chinese Church Voices*, an online project directed by my ChinaSource colleague Joann Pittman, has been an invaluable source for articles, sermons, and social media postings by Christians in China. The very existence of a vibrant online Christian community in China, which provides the source material for *Chinese Church Voices*, is but one evidence of the immense change brought about through the past two decades of massive urbanization. This context of change, providing the backdrop for the unfolding story of China's urban church, is the starting point for a look into the lives of those who are building the city on a hill.

2

The Context for Change

"Come, let us build ourselves a city . . ."[1]

NO OTHER NATION HAS urbanized as rapidly—or on such a large scale—as China. For millennia an agrarian, rural society, China went from being 20 percent urban to having more than half of its people in cities in the space of 30 years. (Britain's urban transformation during the Industrial Revolution, by comparison, took 100 years.) In what is arguably the most massive human migration in the history of the world, China's cities have, since the early 1980s, increased by 500 million people, and they are expected to increase by another 13 million (roughly the size of Tokyo) per year between now and 2030. Urban migrants, now accounting for one-third of the urban population, have flooded to major manufacturing centers in southern and eastern China and to sprawling metropolises that are being reimagined amidst an unprecedented boom of building and redevelopment. These migrants have constructed the Pudong financial center in Shanghai, the iconic "Bird's Nest" stadium and other Olympic venues in Beijing, and countless hotels, office buildings, and condominium towers in cities across China, along with expressways and the new high-speed rail system that is expected to link nearly every city of a half million people or more by the year 2020.[2]

Educational institutions have more than made up for the lost years when they were shuttered during the Cultural Revolution. The number of

1. Genesis 11:4.
2. "Building the Dream."

colleges in China has effectively doubled, and college graduates increased from approximately one million in 1998 to 7.5 million in 2012,[3] Most of China's university students have remained in cities following graduation. For those who went abroad to study, China's burgeoning cities have been magnets of opportunity, particularly when economies in much of the West were declining even as China's own economy continued posting impressive growth figures, some years hitting double digits.

China's geographic transition has had massive social implications, particularly for Chinese families whose identity had, for generations, been tied to the land of their ancestors. Coupled with China's family planning policy, limiting most families to only one child, the widespread dislocation brought about through urbanization signaled the end of the traditional Chinese family as it had been known throughout the dynasties. What Mao had been unable to achieve in his attack upon traditional family structure through the commune system, urbanization has, in many respects, made a reality.

The creation of an urban middle class, roughly the same size as China's urban migrant population, has ushered in a new era of consumerism, making China the number one market for luxury goods globally and making the China market the engine that global business expects will propel the world economy in the coming decades.[4] China's consumer class is important not only for multinationals, but is essential for China itself as it makes a shaky transition from export-led manufacturing to domestic consumption as its major driver of growth. The consumer mentality animates the marketplace of ideas, making it ever more challenging (and resource-intensive) for China's sizeable army of government censors to keep the lid on wide-ranging discussions taking place on the streets and in cyberspace.

Finally, the growing cities serve as China's gateways to the world, drawing a steady stream of business people and students into China while unprecedented numbers of Chinese go abroad as tourists or to study in overseas colleges and, increasingly, high schools. Fueled by China's urban boom, Chinese investment dollars flow to infrastructure projects in Africa and Latin America and snap up companies in the West. One industry group estimates that by the year 2020 Chinese investment in the United States will reach between $100 and $200 billion, accounting for 200,000 to 400,000 American jobs.[5] These three aspects of urbanization—changes in

3. Towson and Woetzel, *The One-Hour China Book.*
4. "Building the Dream."
5 Swanson, "Why China is Buying Up."

the role and structure of the family, the rise of consumerism, and globalization—have reshaped Chinese society, the Chinese church included, bringing a new set of opportunities as well as challenges to China's Christian population.

THE PUSH AND PULL OF URBANIZATION

Urbanization has both a "push" and a "pull" character. For Chinese the "push" has been the lack of economic development in the countryside as compared with the cities, as well as changes in agriculture that have resulted in excess rural labor. The "pull" has been the promise of employment in the cities, along with access to better services, a higher standard of living, and the possibility of making connections that could lead to permanent relocation or even the opportunity to go abroad. In direct opposition to the fluid population flow between countryside and city, however, stands China's household registration, or *hukou,* system. A product of the 1950s, when the government made a conscious decision to limit migration to the cities, the *hukou* system has effectively created two classes of people, rural and urban. Peasants may come to the cities for work, but their official household registration remains in the countryside, thus denying them access to housing, medical benefits, education for their children, and other services guaranteed to urban citizens.

At the national level, the government has been ambivalent about altering this longstanding policy, tacitly allowing the migration to take place while refusing, thus far, to make the sweeping legal changes that would grant peasants equal citizenship. Local governments have been loath to allot tax dollars, and to risk the ire of urban citizens, in order to provide for the needs of migrants, even though these migrants are largely responsible for creating the new urban infrastructure that has allowed China's cities to prosper. As a result social tensions have arisen, with urban residents accusing the peasants of bringing crime and disorder to the cities, while children of urban migrants grow up increasingly bitter and disillusioned by the political and social divide that separates them from realizing the urban dream that surrounds them. Although China has thus far managed to avoid the blight of urban slums that has plagued many other developing nations, without *hukou* reform the current opportunity gap threatens to create a new urban underclass.

For China's Christians, whose ranks swelled in the countryside from the late 1970s to the early 1990s, the push and pull of urbanization have created the impetus not only for physical relocation but also for a rethink of what it means to be the church in 21st century China. As Stark and Wang have pointed out, Christianity in China at the turn of the last century was primarily an urban phenomenon. Although Catholics outnumbered Protestants overall, more Christians in the coastal provinces were Protestant. After 1949, Catholicism declined due to its dependence upon ordained clergy and its organizational loyalty to Rome.[6] Widespread spiritual revival and aggressive church planting by rural believers in the years following Mao's death in 1976 combined to create a spiritual powerhouse in the countryside. A socially marginalized, largely peasant-led movement, the Chinese church, most of it operating outside the government-sanctioned religious structures, was nonetheless a powerful mobilizer of rural youth, many of whom devoted themselves to full-time ministry at an early age and were sent to far-flung villages to plant churches. Today the church's spiritual center of gravity is shifting back to the cities as three distinct streams of Christian influence combine to create a new kind of urban Christian community.

THE GROWING URBAN CHURCH

The peasant migration itself accounts for a significant proportion of China's urban Christians. In cities such as Beijing or Shanghai, they congregate in migrant settlements, usually on the outskirts of the city, often grouped according to their provinces of origin. Large numbers would also be found living on construction sites in the city. In factory towns such as those around Shanghai or in the Pearl River Delta to the south, workers, mostly single women in their late teens or early twenties, live in factory dormitories while working long hours in order to save money to help support their families back home and to provide the means for securing a better life beyond the factory, whether by finding a way to settle down in their newly adopted urban home or by returning to the countryside to engage in small-scale business. Churches of various forms, many led by migrant pastors, have emerged to serve this peasant population. For migrant factory workers, the church may take the form of a regular gathering within the factory, perhaps

---

6. Stark and Wang, *A Star in the East.*

with the blessing of the factory manager, who may be a Christian from Hong Kong or Taiwan.

A very different stream of urban Christians comprises young to middle-aged professionals, many of whom attended university in the city and remained after graduation. Following the crushing of the Tiananmen Square demonstrations in 1989, many students and intellectuals of that era embarked on a spiritual search that grew out of their disillusionment with the government and with their own inability to bring about social and political change. Not a few of these embraced Christianity in the process, becoming outspoken advocates for the faith both in China and abroad. The popularity of Christianity among Chinese intellectuals continued to grow in the 1990s and 2000s. A 2011 survey of students at Beijing's prestigious People's University found that 61.5 percent were "interested" in Christianity.[7]

Stark and Wang attribute Christianity's growth among educated Chinese to a crisis of "cultural incongruity," which they describe as "a conflict between the cultural assumptions of modernity and those of traditional religious culture," resulting in spiritual deprivation. A way of resolving this conflict, seen not only in China but in other urbanizing Asian societies as well, is to reject traditional religions such as Buddhism and to embrace Christianity, which is viewed as better equipped to answer the pressing existential questions brought to light by modernity.[8] As the gospel spread on Chinese university campuses during the 1980s and 1990s, often through the witness of foreign English teachers who were Christians, campus fellowships were formed, which later constituted the nuclei of a new kind of urban congregation. Finally, among Chinese who had gone abroad to study or to work, including many who remained abroad following the failed Tiananmen demonstrations, there emerged a corresponding movement toward the Christian faith. As an increasing number of these have returned, predominately to a handful of larger cities in China, they have contributed their own experience and skills to the leadership of China's emerging urban churches.

These new movements are occurring against the backdrop of an existing urban church under the leadership of the Three-Self Patriotic Movement (TSPM), the officially sanctioned organization charged with overseeing Protestant affairs in China. Quite visible due to the presence

7. Goossaert and Palmer, *The Religious Question in Modern China*, quoted in Stark and Wang, *A Star in the East*, chap. 4.

8. Stark and Wang, *A Star in the East*, chap. 4.

of prominent church buildings scattered around China's major cities, the urban church under the TSPM has not historically had a high degree of influence in the society, both due to the nature of its membership, which, in the early decades of China's reform and opening era, consisted largely of elderly believers who had come to faith before 1949, and due to government-imposed restraints on its activities. However, with the influx of peasant believers as well as the growth of Christianity among young professionals and returnees, these churches are also experiencing rejuvenation and playing an increasingly visible and influential role in urban society. The various types of churches comprising China's contemporary urban Christian community will be explored further in the following chapter.

URBANIZATION 2.0

While China's urbanization generally conjures up images of the towering skylines of Pudong or Shenzhen, the majority of newly urban Chinese will likely end up in smaller cities as part of a phenomenon commonly referred to as Urbanization 2.0. China's urban transformation involves not only megacities, but also the consolidation of small towns across China. Populated mostly by peasants or blue-collar workers, these newly created cities are becoming magnets for those in the countryside who are seeking a better life without having to move to China's coastal metropolises. The look and feel of these third and fourth tier cities is still very rural, although their populations are quite large.

This trend toward developing smaller cities is in keeping with the government's push to modernize agriculture by pursuing efficiency, innovation, more effective land management, sustainable growth, and environmental-friendly farming practices.[9] It also serves to take pressure off larger cities where urban migration is severely stretching infrastructure and causing social tensions. Local governments invest in the relocation of peasants and construction of new rural cities in the expectation that economic activity generated by this newly urbanized consumer class will justify the expense, with excess rural labor being funneled into more productive work, thus closing the gap between urban and rural incomes.

Modernization of the countryside ostensibly brings manufacturing jobs to third and fourth tier cities as these industries move out of higher cost coastal cities, providing opportunities for those leaving the agricultural

9. "China to Speed Up Agri Modernization."

sector. In reality, however, many relocated peasants find themselves saddled with high house payments and few meaningful work opportunities.[10] For peasant Christians, the transition to this urban environment is much more manageable than for those who relocate to the larger cities. Church ministry may be consolidated in terms of geography, as greater numbers of believers may be found in closer proximity to one another, but, in terms of style and practice, it is very similar to that taking place in the countryside.[11]

THE CHANGING SHAPE OF URBAN FAMILIES

China's "one-child" policy has led to several demographic shifts that have significant implications for China's new urban society. Not having grown up with siblings or even cousins of their own, these "only children" may find it difficult to relate to others and may feel less of a need to do so, as the wealth of personal options available in the city means less family or social pressure to conform to traditional norms in personal relationships. Some complain about the weighty expectations of parents and grandparents upon their shoulders; bearing sole responsibility for the extended family's future is a heavy responsibility. One only child told a popular Chinese radio talk show host, "Chinese children are the property of their parents, and we single children, in particular, are the property of all the generations before us."[12] Greater social mobility makes it less likely that a young person will stay in the same city as his or her parents and marry someone within the family relationship network. Although arranged marriages still occur, and for many parents there is the expectation that they will have a role in choosing their son's or daughter's future spouse, in reality singles in China's cities have unprecedented choice in terms of whether or when, and whom, they will marry. An increasing number choose not to, or at least to wait longer before doing so. China's 2010 census revealed that eleven percent of women remained unmarried at age 30, up from 1.2 percent in 2000.[13] Cohabitation before marriage is common, with a 2014 Fudan University survey indicating 43 percent of respondents between ages 25 and 34 had lived together before marriage, compared with only 15 percent in 1989. Professor Li Yinhe of the Chinese Academy of Social Sciences called the

10. Stokols, "China's Rural Urbanization."
11. T. S., interview with author, August 13, 2014.
12. Xinran, *Buy Me the Sky*, quoted in "Only and Lonely."
13. G. J. "Guilt Tripped."

trend "a revolutionary social change," noting that, "Just two decades ago, remaining 'pure before marriage,' was a social norm that everyone in China abided by." Li adds, "As the numbers (of couples living together) rise for each successive generation, even if a man wants a woman who is 'pure' in that sense, he might not be able to find one in China."[14] Living in the city, apart from parents, makes it easier for singles to decide to live together, with or without their parents' knowledge.

Urbanization has also raised the economic and social expectations for those seeking a spouse. *Gao fu shuai* (tall, rich, and handsome) and *bai fu mei* (fair-skinned, rich and beautiful) have become micro blog shorthand for the description of the perfect match. It is said that, without a steady job, a car, and an apartment, a single man in the city has little chance of finding a wife. With the gender imbalance brought about as a result of China's one-child policy, more Chinese men run the risk of not being able to meet the economic requirements for marriage and ending up as "bare branches," a slang term referring to men over a certain age who have not been able to marry and thus, like a branch without leaves, have no wife and no children. A host of online dating sites has emerged to cater to China's urban singles, providing a digital-era solution to their dilemma while playing upon traditional feelings about the need to marry in order to pressure users into signing up.

The nuclear family has replaced "three generations under one roof" as the dominate image of the urban household, due both to the disappearance of large extended families and the practicalities of housing in China's cities. At the same time, however, children of the "one-child" generation who themselves have children may enlist the help of their parents if they are in the same city or if a parent is willing to relocate, at least temporarily, to assist with child-rearing duties while the parents themselves continue pursuing their careers. As in other rapidly developing cities, marital problems and divorce have emerged as major social issues.

The "one-child" policy coupled with the traditional preference for male children has also contributed to a skewed gender ratio. For every 100 females born in China, there are 119 boys. In some provinces the ratio is as high as 135:100.[15] As this generation has reached marrying age and beyond, the specter has emerged of as many as 30 million men in China who will be unable to find wives.

14. Chang, "More Unwed Couples."
15. "Gender Imbalance in China."

Finally, as China's birth rates have been brought under control during the past three decades the number of working-age people as a percentage of the total population has begun to plateau and will decrease steadily over the next decade. Meanwhile the proportion of China's elderly has begun to mushroom. The pyramid-shaped demographic profile that characterized China up through the 1970s, with a large pool of children and youth at the bottom and a comparatively smaller elderly population at the top, is rapidly being replaced by a barrel-shaped contour featuring a large middle-aged population that is steadily moving into the ranks of the elderly. Today there are more than 200 million senior citizens in China. Of these some 30 million are considered disabled. As of 2012 there were only 3.9 million nursing home beds available in all of China. By 2050 the elderly population is estimated to reach 400 million, accounting for a third of the country's total population.[16] Given the traditional expectation that the young are to take care of their older relatives, as well as the lack of a suitable social safety net to meet the needs of China's burgeoning older population, the burden that this demographic reality places upon the urban infrastructure is for-midable. As will be seen in the following chapters, China's growing elderly population, along with the gender imbalance and the personal and family issues faced by the "only child" generation, place unique pressures upon the urban church as well.

CHINA'S SECOND ECONOMIC TRANSITION

Having successfully overseen the development of China as "the world's fac-tory floor," enabling the country to enjoy decades of export-led economic growth, China's leaders now face the even more formidable task of turn-ing the country's emerging urban consumer class into the nation's new economic engine. Researchers at McKinsey Consulting see the Chinese consumer as pivotal; the question is whether consumer demand will be sufficient to allow China to maintain growth levels near the eight percent per year that is believed necessary to keep unemployment at manageable levels while avoiding recession.[17] Making this transition even more difficult is the exit of manufacturing jobs from China and the widespread introduc-tion of robotic technology in the factories that remain, further reducing the need for low-skill labor.

16. Yao, "Golden Years."
17. Huang, "China's Great Rebalancing."

China's state-run sector is undergoing consolidation in an effort to make profitable those state-owned enterprises (SOEs) that survived the shakeout that began in the 1990s. Government jobs are becoming less attractive. Meanwhile, slow growth in the developed world focuses more attention on China as the one bright spot that could potentially fuel a global recovery. Again quoting McKinsey, "Most large consumer-facing companies realize they will need China to power their growth in the next decade."[18] China's growing middle class appears to be rising to the occasion, fueling markets for everything from private automobiles and luxury handbags to overseas travel. The "one-child" policy has put a premium on education, traditionally a priority in Chinese families, with parents competing to place their only children in prestigious schools, beginning with kindergarten, and prepared to invest a large proportion of the couple's income in tuition up through and including college. Overseas recruiters are finding a fertile market in China among families eager to send their one child to the United States for high school or college.

Whether China's urban consumer class can successfully bear the load of the "second economic transition" remains to be seen. As of this writing, the strains of making this transition are already evident as China faces significant economic slowdown, a growing gap between rich and poor, the threat of rising unemployment, and an exodus of capital and talent from the country, all of which pose a formidable challenge to a regime that has staked its legitimacy on its ability to guarantee continued economic prosperity.

A LOOMING ENVIRONMENTAL CRISIS

Exacerbating this economic challenge is the environmental degradation that has accompanied China's rapid urbanization and headlong pursuit of economic growth. Beijing's poor air quality, with pollutant levels on some days so high that they cannot be measured, has become legendary and is emblematic of the situation in many Chinese cities. Each year an estimated 1.2 million people in China die prematurely as a result of air pollution.[19] Most of this is the result of China's heavy reliance on coal, which accounts for nearly 70% of its total energy consumption.[20] As of 2013 less than

18. Atsmon and Magni, "Meet the Chinese Consumer."
19. Chen, "Life Expectancy," 9.
20. Andrews-Speed, "China's Energy," 10.

one percent of China's largest 500 cities met World Health Organization criteria for clear air.[21] That same year government sources reported that the groundwater of 90 percent of cities was polluted, 60 percent of these severely.[22] More than forty percent of China's arable land is degraded as a result of erosion and the effects of polluting chemicals, and up to forty percent of China's rivers are severely polluted.[23, 24] In the words of one researcher, "These various data points reinforce the simple but chilling message that the inputs on which human life depends (food, water, and air) have become toxic to Chinese citizens in numerous ways."[25]

The stress on the environment will only grow worse as China continues to urbanize, as those in the cities consume four times more energy and 2.5 times more water per capita than their rural counterparts.[26] The growing urban middle and upper classes have also contributed to environmental degradation globally through their purchases of ivory and of other rare animal products that are sought for their supposed medicinal qualities, hastening the demise of some of the world's most endangered species. Some hoard these commodities with an eye toward the day when these species will be extinct, causing the value of their investment to skyrocket.[27]

China's environmental crisis is the result of decades of prioritizing economic growth, and the acquisition of energy resources to feed that growth, over concerns about the long-term health of its citizens. As both the world's largest producer of greenhouse gases and the leading consumer of energy resources, China's response to its own ecological calamity has global implications. In response to increasing grassroots as well as international pressure, China's leaders have begun to take deliberate action. Premier Li Keqiang has "declared war" on pollution, and President Xi Jinping has taken the lead in supporting measures such as the Action Plan for the Prevention and Control of Air Pollution.[28] Given the relatively weak status of China's environmental regulatory structures, along with tight state control and a host of vested interests in the energy sector, the structural change needed

21. Economy, "China's Environmental Future."
22. Van Wyk, "Groundwater."
23. Patton, "China's Arable Land."
24. Economy, "China's Environmental Future."
25. Shobert, "Key Drivers," 49–50.
26. Economy, "China's Environmental Future."
27. Platt, "China's Wealthy."
28. Shobert, "Key Drivers," 48.

to realize genuine environmental reform will likely be difficult and slow in coming. As China moves aggressively to meet ambitious targets for reducing carbon emissions, however, its overall energy mix is starting to shift, with coal use starting to decline. In 2014 the amount of coal-produced electricity fell for the first time since 1974, while electricity from alternative energy sources increased by 20 percent.[29] China has become the world leader in hardware for harnessing renewable energy, such as solar panels and wind turbines. The capacity to produce such equipment has thus far outstripped the country's ability to use the resulting clean energy, however, due to piecemeal policy implementation and an emphasis on manufacturing over adapting existing energy infrastructure such as power grids.[30]

For the foreseeable future China's need for imported fuel will continue to increase its global presence, opening the door for potentially greater cooperation with other nations in energy production and delivery but also increasing the likelihood of competition for scarce resources, resulting in new diplomatic and potentially military challenges.[31] The very real needs for energy, water and other resources, and the concomitant impact of urbanization upon the environment, have far-reaching domestic and international implications that are shared by China's Christians as they grapple with the question of what it means to be responsible stewards of creation in an era when food and water security are among the most critical global issues.

THE MARKETPLACE OF IDEAS

With the rise of the urban consumer class comes greater personal choice, not only in financial decisions but also in matters of lifestyle and belief. As long as one does not venture into the forbidden area of politics, the marketplace of ideas is open in urban China. For China's Christians, this marketplace provides a legitimate forum in which to proclaim their beliefs. It also introduces new competition, whether from traditional Chinese religions such as Buddhism or folk practices, Confucianism, or other forms of spirituality.

Although officially atheistic, China's ruling Communist Party has significantly relaxed its grip on ideology since the inauguration of the reform and opening policy in the early 1980s. In theory religion is to be contained

29. "China Smog War."
30. Andrews-Speed, "China's Energy," 12.
31. Herberg, "China's Search," 20, 27.

within the officially sanctioned structures (in the case of Protestant Christians, the Three-Self Patriotic Movement) provided for this purpose. In practice, a large gray area has emerged during the past three decades in which a wide variety of religious practices are tolerated. These practices include unregistered Christian house meetings, which, in China's cities, have grown to include gatherings of up to several hundred people meeting in rented facilities. Also included are various types of schools—registered or otherwise—run by religious groups, the legal publication of books with religious content, and the involvement of religious believers in charity activities. Although not protected by law and thus subject to censure at the hands of unsympathetic officials, these activities have become increasingly common with the growth of China's urban civil society.

Of particular significance for China's urban Christians is the growth of online religious activity that has accompanied China's rapid and enthusiastic adoption of the Internet. Despite much talk about China's "great firewall," engineered to screen offending content from outside China, a plethora of religious content is being generated domestically. Online Christian newspapers, magazines, individual church sites, e-commerce outlets, Christian dating clubs, seminary courses, plus tens of thousands of individual blogs and millions of micro blog users, combine to create a vibrant online Christian community in China. Largely unregulated, this community brings together Christians from across the country, overcoming barriers of distance and government regulation that had, in the past, prevented large numbers of believers from associating with one another. It has also enabled the establishment of a Christian "brand," within the marketplace of ideas, where Christian content can be shaped to fit the demands of the market and freely dispensed and discussed among China's rapidly growing online population.

ENTERING THE GLOBAL COMMUNITY

China's cities have long been key to its policy of opening to the outside world, serving as centers for commerce, education, and cultural exchange. Special Economic Zones such as Shenzhen in the south provided laboratories for new policies that would eventually be implemented nationwide. By selectively limiting over time which parts of the country were open to foreign nationals, the government has been able largely to contain their presence and influence in China's major cities. In the future, enhanced transportation links with China's neighbors will further bolster the strategic role of cities, not only the traditionally influential metropolises along the eastern seaboard but also emerging megacities in China's ethnic minority regions that will provide a needed interface with Southeast and Central Asia and beyond. President Xi Jinping's "one belt, one road" strategy envisions a revival of the ancient Silk Road that two thousand years ago linked China and its trading partners in Europe. Consisting of high-speed rail lines along with highways and oil and gas pipelines, this transportation infrastructure would ostensibly provide a counterbalance to China's current reliance on maritime routes, which could potentially be choked off in the event of a military conflict. China's strategy for the massive transportation and trade link includes "infrastructure diplomacy," namely, strengthening relations with countries along the route, including the Central Asian republics, Vietnam and Myanmar, through investment. Encompassing 4.4 billion people with a combined GDP equal to one-third of the world's wealth, the new Silk Road would eventually link China to three continents. In the words of one analyst, "If this vision can be fulfilled, then eventually all roads will quite literally lead to Beijing."[32]

As gateways to the outside world, China's cities provide a point of connection as well between Chinese Christians and the global Christian community. In the early years of China's opening most foreign Christians were congregated in a few large cities, while the majority of Chinese believers were found in the countryside. Interaction between the two was sporadic and often risky. Even in the officially sanctioned urban churches interaction between foreign and local Christians was rare. With the emergence of an increasingly cosmopolitan urban Christian community as well as the influx of hundreds of thousands of overseas Chinese, who often play a "bridge" function between local Chinese and non-Chinese in China, interaction between the indigenous church and the global Christian community has become frequent and multidimensional.

In this context the roles of foreign Christians are changing, bringing new possibilities for collaboration between Christians inside and outside China. Whereas in the past foreign Christians might have been expected to provide needed biblical training for Chinese pastors who had no formal theological background or to be directly involved in evangelism among students or business contacts who had never met a Chinese Christian, today they are more likely to serve the Chinese church in a behind-the-scenes

32. Rolland, "China's New Silk Road."

mentoring or encouragement role while Chinese Christians take the lead in overt Christian activities.

As urban believers, for example, wrestle with how to model their faith within the complex and often inhospitable environment of China's cities, foreign Christians can offer suggestions growing out of their own experiences in countries where the Christian presence is more fully developed, particularly in its engagement with society. Together they can assess problems affecting the church and how best to address these given the resources available within the Chinese Christian community itself. Chinese and foreign Christian professionals in fields ranging from education to engineering can naturally interact in the workplace as they work out the implications of their faith for their respective vocations. Christian business leaders can together face the challenge of operating ethically in the commercial world where corruption is endemic and under-the-table dealings are taken for granted. In the absence of older Christian role models within the emerging urban churches, seasoned Christians from abroad can play an important role by way of example in their marriages and family lives.

Although government restrictions on foreign non-profit entities, particularly in the area of religion, effectively limit formal relationships between Christian groups inside and outside China, the cities provide a somewhat safe place where such relationships can at least be explored, paving the way for deeper interaction and collaboration if and when the political environment should change to allow it. All of these connections, which would have been difficult if not inconceivable thirty years ago, are now possible by virtue of China's urbanization and the emergence of today's urban Christian community.

NO GOING BACK

The context of urbanization provides the new environment in which China's church currently finds itself. While the church is still very much in transition, and the future of urban Christianity in China in many ways uncertain, it is clear that there is no going back. As China's geographic and social landscape has been indelibly redrawn by the forces of urbanization, so China's church is being transformed as it answers the question of what it means to be the church in the city. Doing so requires new forms of worship and ministry, new structures, and new roles. In the following chapter we look at the ways in which China's Christians are seeking to adapt to their new urban environment.

3

New Wineskins

"And no one puts new wine into old wineskins . . ."[1]

THE WIDESPREAD REVIVAL THAT the church in China enjoyed during the late 1970s and 1980s following the death of Mao Zedong was primarily a rural phenomenon, taking place largely through the multiplication of unregistered house churches, although newly opened churches under the reconstituted Three Self Patriotic Movement, which had ceased to function during the Cultural Revolution, also experienced growth.[2] Since no new pastors had been trained since the mid-1950s, the rural house churches were led by laity, usually peasant farmers or young persons, most of them female, who were commissioned and sent out to plant churches in other villages. Although several large networks emerged, led by strong charismatic leaders, individual congregations themselves remained rather decentralized, aligning with one or another network at different times depending on needs and circumstances. Sporadic persecution at the hands of local officials required these congregations to remain mobile, ready to change location at a moment's notice. Security concerns, as well as China's lagging communications and transportation infrastructure, kept church leaders from interacting with one another.

Regular local gatherings took place in homes, while larger revival meetings were held in secluded rural locations, often for days at a time. Signs

1. Luke 5:37.
2. Lambert, *China's Christian Millions.*

and miracles accompanied the preaching of the gospel, with the majority of believers claiming that their own conversions were due to instances of miraculous healing or demonic deliverance.[3] The fundamentalist theology of these congregations, influenced both by the pietism of foreign entities such as the China Inland Mission as well as early twentieth century millennial movements, emphasized being born again, repentance, separation from the world, personal holiness, the primacy of evangelism, a loving community, and preparation for Christ's imminent return. Evangelists preached the pathway of the cross, a message of suffering that included being willing to face poverty, eat bitterness (*chiku,*), and face death for the gospel's sake. The church relied upon sympathetic believers outside China for Bibles and theological training, and often for financial support for evangelists as well.

The dynamic yet fragmented, widespread yet socially marginalized peasant movement that characterized China's Christian revival in the closing decades of the last century has gradually given way to a new form of church that represents, in some respects, the antithesis of China's rural house church. The external forces of urbanization, and internal changes within, are moving the church geographically, from the countryside to the cities, and socially, from the fringes of society into the mainstream. Church leadership has become better educated and more professional. As they move from survival mode toward developing a sense of social mandate, China's Christians are finding new ways to connect their eternal vision to the practical needs of those outside the church. Dependence upon outside resources has given way to partnership as the church in China finds its place within the global Christian community.

MAPPING THE URBAN CHURCH LANDSCAPE

While the term "urban church" generally denotes emerging faith communities that exhibit several or all of the characteristics listed above, significant differences exist between various types of churches found in China's cities. In their study of Beijing churches, Ying, Yuan, and Lao documented four distinct types: those affiliated with the TSPM, those composed of believers from the eastern Chinese city of Wenzhou, migrant churches, and urban professional churches.[4] According to Liu and Wang, this latter type, the "urban newly formed churches" (*chengshi xinxing jiaohui*), had mostly

3. Conkling, *Mobilized Merchants-Patriotic Martyrs,* chap. 2.
4. Ying et al., "Civic Communities," 82.

been founded since 2000, are composed largely of relatively new Christians in their 30s, and average around 50 in attendance. These congregations have full-time pastors, although they are not paid particularly well, and they meet in rented facilities rather than in homes.[5]

The migrant churches, sometimes referred to as "the rural church in the city," often have roots in rural house church movements, although the younger leadership responsible for these urban congregations tends to see them not merely as transplants from the countryside, but as a new kind of Christian community that needs to develop according to its urban environment. Those rural movements that have embraced the city and adjusted their strategy to fit the urban context have managed this transition fairly well, while those that have insisted on maintaining their former traditions have faced difficulty.[6] These migrant pastors generally serve multiple congregations, which remain somewhat fluid due to the nomadic nature of migrant life. As the city moves outward and migrant neighborhoods face redevelopment, the whole congregation may need to pick up and relocate several miles away.

The Wenzhou churches, originating from the eponymous city in China's eastern Zhejiang province that is famous both for its economic prosperity as well as a high proportion of religious believers, occupy a unique place on today's urban Christian landscape. Isolated by high mountains and having its own distinct dialect, Wenzhou has enjoyed a relatively high degree of freedom due to a "hands-off" policy by the central government (which shifted significantly in 2014 when a provincial crackdown on church structures resulted in several church buildings being demolished and crosses being removed from hundreds more). Wenzhou's status as a hotbed of Christian activity has been marked by the dominance of "boss Christian" leaders who travel throughout China and beyond to open new markets for Wenzhou goods and to plant Wenzhou-style churches.

To these four types may be added a fifth, namely, traditional unregistered urban house churches whose history dates back to the 1950s or before and which reemerged in the late 1970s following the Cultural Revolution. While similar in leadership structure and theological orientation to China's rural house churches, these traditional urban churches have generally enjoyed greater stability, often meeting in the same home for a long period

---

5. Liu and Wang, *Guankan Zhongguo Chengshi Jiating Jiaohui*, quoted in Wielander, *Christian Values*, 16-17.

6. Yuan Hao, interview with author, July 22, 2014.

of time, and have benefited from having leaders who were comparatively better educated, some having received formal theological training in the 1940s or 1950s.

The primary focus of the present study is the newly emerging urban professional churches, although reference will be made to other types as well. While the trends within this emerging stream suggest significant new directions for the church, it should be noted that these are not assumed to be uniform across the entire urban church, which exhibits considerable diversity within its ranks. Nevertheless, by looking at some of the early adaptors described in the following pages it is possible to discern how the Chinese Christian community is changing as its members seek to adapt to, and function within, a new urban environment.

A CHURCH IN TRANSITION

A Christian who grew up in a house church and later went abroad to study encapsulated many of the dynamics that characterize the church's urban transition as he contrasted the church culture of the past with that of urban churches today:

> Back then there was real persecution and a real price to pay. People had a real faith, a real experiential relationship with Christ and dependence on him, and a real spirituality. There was not as much formal theological training, but the informal influence of the "pillar" doctrines. Now we have systematic training. People know a lot but lack the spiritual wisdom and penetrating power that comes out of persecution. In the past, leaders naturally emerged, with a desire to serve, and the older generation encouraged them to serve. Today some leaders are home-grown, but others are self-appointed, or they came out of college fellowships with no real church background. Leaders in the past had spiritual authority, so people followed them. They learned from the older generation. There was not a high degree of organization so it was very easy to start from spiritual fellowship and to go deep in relationship.
>
> Now we have many different cultures in the church, and different theological backgrounds. Some are ministry-driven; some are theologically driven. Now we start with ministry [rather than fellowship] and from there have to gradually go deeper to heart issues. Before we had no ordination, but a large family atmosphere and a sense of communion. Everyone did the ministry. Now there are more formal relationships, emphasizing the pastor's authority

over the believers. The congregation obeys the pastor, most of whom are full-time, and the pastor drives the ministry in a top-down style. . . . Finally, the church used to be persecuted by the society and socially marginalized by political power, with very little opportunity for social involvement. Now it's more complicated. No one persecutes you or marginalizes you, but you have more opportunity. Yet the prevailing value system pulls you away from your faith; it's very easy to forget you're a Christian because you fit in with the rest of the society.[7]

Both generational differences and the practical realities of a new urban setting are driving structural change in China's church. Traditional rural house church networks tended to be defined by geography, distinctive worship practices, or personalities.[8] The large networks originating out of Henan or Anhui, for example, were identified with the counties in which they originated and, although they gained nationwide influence, retained much of the character of those places. Pastoral leadership was often concentrated in the hands of a few of the top leader's relatives, who would assume collective responsibility for decision making, particularly during times when the top leader was in prison. Given the rapid growth and fluid nature of the rural networks, there was little felt need for sophisticated structure or for written policies and procedures. What was lacking in organization was made up for by relationship; members enjoyed intimate fellowship as they returned periodically to the training sites from which they had been sent out to plant churches. These sites became connecting points where these itinerant evangelists would give reports, often replete with stories of miraculous healings and mass conversions, thus fueling the zeal and further fanning the flames of revival within the movement.[9]

Absent this "family" tradition nurtured by larger-than-life top leaders and by events—such as training conferences—which helped to solidify commitment among members, China's emerging urban congregations are struggling to find suitable structures to address the limitations and difficulties that emerge with growth. Although the rural and urban contexts are very different, Christians from traditional house church backgrounds are, at least in some respects, better able to meet the challenges of growth than are those who have no such frame of reference. At the same time, the urban

7. W. E., interview with author, July 13, 2014.

8. Wu, "Authority," 12.

9. Y. R., interview with author, July 9, 2014.

constraints of space and time, as well as the changing nature of those within the church, make the traditional organizational pattern unworkable in this new setting.

According to one Chinese Christian intellectual, the very future of the church in China depends upon the church's ability to change its outmoded leadership structure: "To exist and develop in China, Christianity must begin to change itself, namely to realize two changes: to move from the edge to the center of the society; and to change from the management model of individual responsibility by church leaders to a collective management model of democratic supervision. Without these two changes, there is no future for Christianity in China."[10]

Not all Christians in China would agree with this observation. Some would emphasize that it is the gospel message itself, not the church's management model, which will ultimately attract people into the church. Others would dismiss the notion of the church moving toward the center of society as wishful thinking or would question to what extent the church ought to be concerned with its role in society. Differences around these issues characterize much of the current debate among China's urban Christians.

CHANGING EXPECTATIONS

In their study of urban churches, Ying et al. found, in both TSPM and unregistered congregations, a correlation between structure and member participation.[11] With a lessening of the stigma associated with church involvement in the cities has come the phenomenon of casual church attendance, resulting in a rate of high turnover from week to week and month to month. Beginning in the mid- to late 2000s, urban unregistered congregations began to adopt formal membership procedures and requirements in order encourage a higher degree of commitment.[12] They are increasingly willing to practice church discipline in dealing with members. Management teams came into being in order to provide financial accountability as larger sums of money were needed to pay pastors and to rent facilities. Compared with rural churches, urban congregations put more of an emphasis on formal commitment, both for leaders as well as members. China Gospel Fellowship, a large network originally based in Henan province,

10. Huo, "Two Transformations."
11. Ying et al., "Civic Communities," 96–97.
12. Mary Ma, interview with author, August 15, 2014.

began ordaining pastors in 2000. Prior to that time the church had only "uncles," or top leaders, and co-workers (*tonggong*).[13]

The realities of urban church growth and the character, status, and qualifications of China's urban Christians point to the need for power to devolve from a handful of top leaders to the congregation. Urban Christians tend to be more highly educated and possess a broad range of work experience; as a result they have more to offer the church by way of their expertise and they bring higher expectations for meaningful involvement in church affairs. This is particularly true of those who have studied abroad or have participated in churches outside China. These lay people see themselves as "stakeholders" and demand a role in decision making. Rather than waiting for leaders to launch new programs and tell the congregation how it is to be involved, today's urban believers are more likely to see needs within the church or the community and to initiate new ministries themselves.[14] Ying et al. cite Beijing's Shouwang Church as an example of a congregation that has a high degree of participation in programs, as well as in decisions regarding the church's organization and direction. In the words of one Shouwang member, "When we demand democracy from the government, the church should practice democracy in the first place."[15]

With the influx of teaching from outside China, the church is also undergoing a theological shift that affects how believers view their involvement. Mainstream Chinese theology, much of it heavily influenced by indigenous church leader and theologian Watchman Nee, traditionally emphasized personal piety and the individual devotional life, giving rise to a privatized faith. New teaching on the church, including that which is coming out of the Reformed tradition, brings a well-developed ecclesiology that sets forth systematically the responsibilities of church members. In some congregations the intentional involvement of leaders from outside China provides the impetus for lay involvement. Pastors from Hong Kong, Taiwan, or Korea, for example, have launched unregistered congregations with the goal of nurturing a local team of believers to carry on the work. This "build-operate-transfer" model has resulted in a number of new congregations being established in southern China's Pearl River Delta region and elsewhere.

13. Yuan Hao, interview with author, July 22, 2014.

14. Kim-kwong Chan, interview with author, July 4, 2014.

15. Ying et al., "Civic Communities," 95.

LEADERSHIP IN TRANSITION

While the trend toward greater participation bodes well for the future vitality of the urban church, a lack of concrete procedures for participatory management and of relevant role models of servant leadership leave the church groping haltingly in its efforts to move forward. Church leaders in the 1980s, who had received theological training before 1949 and who had survived the darkest years of persecution under Mao, possessed solid biblical knowledge, experience, and deep spiritual passion. The succeeding generation, largely rural, was schooled in the classroom of suffering. They earned their positions within rapidly growing unregistered networks through their willingness to serve and gained the respect of other leaders by virtue of the size of their networks. In the hierarchical church structures they developed, unquestioned obedience was the norm. While younger workers under them may have been trained to take on various portions of the work, no thought was given to succession planning. In many cases relatives of the senior leader held top leadership positions, creating a further barrier to younger leaders moving up through the ranks.

In his study of Chinese church ecclesiology, Jackson Wu contrasts traditional leadership characteristics found among Chinese pastors with the attributes of contemporary Western leaders: "In Chinese culture, tradition and social position hold sway. In modern times, reason, experience, and the autonomous individual form a triumvirate in the West . . . Similarly, in more urban, wealthy, and educated settings, one sees a loosening of traditional authoritarianism, identification with parents, and ties to ancestral land . . ."[16] Based in Confucian thinking regarding authority, leadership has traditionally been seen as deriving from position, regardless of the abilities of the leader. The resulting strong authoritarianism is balanced with personal benevolence; in return for their unquestioning loyalty those under leadership can expect that the leader will behave kindly toward them. This leadership is inherently conservative, basing its actions on a commonly accepted notion of correct behavior that is rooted in history, and it is risk averse.

BREAKING THE MOLD

Yuan Hao, a scholar who has studied extensively the transformation of China Gospel Fellowship from a rural-based to an urban-focused network,

16. Wu, "Authority," 6–7.

notes that, although church networks are moving away from family rule (*jiazhang zhi*) and toward empowering individual congregations, within the congregation itself the leaders may still use *jiazhang zhi* approach.[17] Ying et al. looked at the failures of two different migrant congregations in Beijing to reach consensus, one regarding relocation and the other, a Wenzhou church plant, regarding whether the church should localize. The congregation in the first instance "was limited by its structure and its inability to mobilize believers." Leaders were reluctant to engage with members in discussing controversial issues, and the church lacked a way for members to air views and reach a consensus. The members likewise had a difficult time expressing and discussing their opinions.[18]

Urban church leaders in China are mindful, and often critical, of the traditional authoritarian leadership mold and its effects upon the church. The notion of leadership is beginning to shift from being defined by position to being defined by influence.[19] With greater professionalization in leadership, exposure to leadership patterns from other cultures, rising sophistication among urban believers, and greater scrutiny from the society at large, has come a self-conscious effort to rethink church leadership. Although the new urban congregations may have democratic structures, such as elected committees, leadership can still be autocratic, creating tension between the ideal and reality. Lacking role models who demonstrate a viable alternative, church leaders fall back on social norms, unconsciously adopting contemporary political leaders and structures as models of leadership because "that's how we've been brought up," even though they acknowledge that these ingrained structures and behaviors fall short of the biblical standard for relationships within the church.[20]

Otto Lui, in his research on mentoring practices among church leaders, found that, once church members realized the fallacy of their concept that only one person could be a leader, they were then left to deal with the conflicts and power struggles that occurred as people learned to work together as a team. With the higher education level of believers in the cities comes a greater likelihood that a group of believers will emerge that is able to successfully work through these issues.[21] Even so, while Christians may

17. Yuan Hao, interview with author, July 22, 2014.
18. Ying et al., "Civic Communities," 89, 91.
19. Otto Lui, interview with author, July 14, 2014.
20. Mary Ma, interview with author, August 15, 2014.
21. Otto Lui, interview with author, July 14, 2014.

give lip service to the concept of team leadership, their default mode may still be to look for a very strong individual to lead the team. "Team" in their minds may be a group of people who are delegated to carry out tasks, but who do not function as a genuine team.

The authoritarian mindset, learned from the examples of hierarchical church leaders (including modern-day urban megachurches in China, Korea or the West) or gleaned from China's prevailing political culture, has yet to change. In the words of one overseas Chinese pastor who has worked extensively with the unregistered church in China, "New structures and organizational arrangements are being put into place, but, absent a change in mindset, the result is legalism, not the restoration of relationships."[22] Given these shortcomings, Ying et al. concluded that, "Even if political control were to decrease Chinese churches would have to do more to achieve a higher level of autonomy and good governance."[23]

The tension is more acute within the traditional urban churches and in some TSPM congregations, where dynastic leadership extending back multiple generations may rely on lengthy sermons and forced study and memorization to enforce their authority, leaving little room for younger leaders who may have different ideas about how to run the church. TSPM leaders may also be engaged in long-running bureaucratic battles over issues such as church property, and not up to facing the new challenges posed by a younger and rapidly changing congregation.[24]

A NEW GENERATION

The generation of urban leaders that has emerged during the past decade, composed of those currently in their 40s and 50s, has been marked by a relatively high level of biblical knowledge, a pragmatism that has made it possible to work effectively across a complex social and political landscape, and a willingness to adopt new ideas and practices. Many come from professional or business backgrounds and bring into their ministry roles the lessons learned from their past work experience. Unlike their rural predecessors, who were known for building large networks, these leaders are, for the most part, building individual congregations, although they may see part of their role as connecting with others leaders such as themselves

22. L. D., interview with author, July 7, 2014.

23. Ying et al., "Civic Communities," 101.

24. Andrew Kaiser, interview with author, July 22, 2014.

for the purpose of outreach into the community or cross-cultural mission sending. While, in the TSPM-affiliated churches, it is common to find pastors who come from Christian families, leaders in the unregistered congregations are often first-generation Christians who found themselves thrust into ministry within the first few years following conversion.

Observers of this generation have pointed out that, in many cases, the personal spiritual development of these leaders has not kept pace with the growth of the churches they have pioneered, often due to the high demands placed upon them by their congregations, leaving little space for personal growth. Some see in their pragmatism an unhealthy instrumentalism that has made them extremely task-oriented. The early success and rapid advancement of their work has resulted in unrealistic expectations; to satisfy the demands and diverse needs of their increasingly sophisticated congregations they raise the bar high, both for themselves and for the staff and volunteers under their leadership. Although they may have demonstrated through their accomplishments their abilities as leaders, they may not feel qualified to mentor those under them, nor do they have time to do so. Instead, they may seek outside study opportunities, including programs overseas, as a means of developing leaders.[25]

One younger pastor from a second tier Chinese city commented that those belonging to the current generation of pioneering urban unregistered church leaders are basically victims of their own success. Many of these leaders have been able to make a mark on their communities by founding fairly large congregations in the face of government regulations that, at least in theory, forbid their existence. In doing so they have placed themselves in opposition to the government—similar to many of the prominent rural unregistered church leaders who emerged in 1980s—some to the point of becoming openly antagonistic. Like their rural predecessors, their success has relied to varying degrees upon support from outside China in the form of training resources, mentoring, encouragement, denominational affiliation, or financial contributions. Unlike most of the previous generation, these leaders have benefited from formal theological training, which has provided legitimacy within the community and has contributed the doctrinal and structural underpinnings of their ministries.

According to this younger pastor, these success factors now inhibit the further development of the urban church. In addition to requiring significant resources for their ongoing operations, large churches do not allow for

25. Otto Lui, interview with author, July 14, 2014.

the development of intimate relationships among believers. Their structures perpetuate the top-down hierarchical style of leadership that stifled the development of younger leadership in the traditional rural networks. These urban leaders' stance vis-à-vis the government makes it more difficult for them to work within official limits in the future and makes it less likely that their congregations will eventually receive government recognition. Their antagonism also raises a red flag for those in their communities who may otherwise be interested in joining the church, making it difficult for these leaders to engage effectively with society. Similarly, the foreign connections of these leaders raise suspicions about their motives, particularly as the current regime appears increasingly anti-Western in its outlook. Finally, the same theological frameworks that have given structure to their ministries can become a straitjacket, preventing these leaders from considering contrasting ideas and thus limiting their exposure to, and relationships with, other leaders with whom they might otherwise collaborate. Thus, although leaders of the current generation are very different from their predecessors, these leaders nonetheless exhibit, albeit in different ways, some of the same limitations of the previous generation.[26]

An overseas Chinese pastor who has spent much of the past three decades working with pastors in China has identified five gaps in the lives of today's church leaders. Due to a lack of positive encouragement during their growing up years, they become demotivated when faced with harsh and unrealistic expectations from superiors or from their congregations, resulting in low self-esteem. A lack of personal direction, particularly for pioneering urban pastors, leaves them without an understanding of how to shepherd their congregations. Only when they experience the patient guidance of a shepherd are they able to patiently shepherd others. Brought up in an environment where communication between leaders and followers is generally one-way, leaders lack the ability to receive needed feedback from others who could help them to see their own blind spots. Similarly, the traditional social distance between leaders and followers stands in the way of leaders developing genuine friendships. Finally, while persecution often exposes the vulnerabilities of leaders, these leaders tend to feel isolated and alone when under pressure. In order to address these gaps, this trainer suggests that the traditional Confucian model of leader development, emphasizing position and knowledge, needs to be replaced by a mentoring model that will provide living examples to church leaders, allow them to receive

26. L. J., interview with author, January 22, 2014.

input from others, and that will offer the emotional support needed to endure pressures both within the community of believers and externally.[27]

PROFESSIONALIZATION

With urbanization has come professionalization of church leadership. Following the reconstitution of the TSPM and the formation of the China Christian Council in 1980, Bible schools began to be reopened under the auspices of the CCC. There are currently 20 such institutions in operation, with a total student body at any given time of around 1500. Only one school, the Union Theological Seminary in Nanjing, offers a graduate-level program. These institutions have been supplemented by hundreds of training programs offered by individual TSPM churches, primarily for rural pastors and lay leaders, which are staffed variously by pastors from the host church, visiting faculty from a CCC Bible school, or guest instructors from outside China.

While full-time, trained pastors may be common in many TSPM congregations, most unregistered church leaders have traditionally been bi-vocational and lacked formal theological training. Leaders rose to their positions, not necessarily because they were qualified, but because of charisma, personal relationships, age, or, in the case of Wenzhou's "boss Christians," financial status.[28] Whatever training they had received was often haphazard, depending upon the availability of visiting teachers or upon the limited teaching resources within their particular networks.

Rural unregistered churches began developing training programs in the early 1980s, often with the assistance of visiting Christians from abroad. Some incorporated systematic seminary training programs broadcast via shortwave from outside China or cassette tapes carried into China and duplicated for distribution among churches. In this situation, standardization was next to impossible, as the menu of offerings varied greatly by network or individual training center. Courses with identical names might have been taught in one context by a visiting seminary professor from the United States using a translator and, in another instance, by a local pastor with a junior high school education whose own theological training had been received via shortwave radio broadcasts from Taiwan or Hong Kong.

27. Lee, "Mentoring."
28. Ying et al., "Civic Communities," 89.

More sophisticated programs involving students from multiple house church networks emerged in the 1990s, most of which were based in larger cities and relied on a stream of visiting faculty from abroad to provide the bulk of the instruction. Teaching in these institutions has evolved from a traditional emphasis on biblical knowledge and ministry skills to a more interactive, student-based approach combining classroom instruction with discussion, mentorship, and practical experience through internships. Since the early 2000s, several Western theological institutions have been providing Internet-based courses, with local proctors in China grading papers and conducting tutorials with students. Chinese preparing for ministry have increasingly been able to go abroad for studies. Several schools in Asia and North America have programs specifically for Mainland Chinese students, some conducted entirely in Mandarin. Finally, with the emergence of Christian studies centers at nearly three dozen Chinese universities, some church leaders have been able to obtain undergraduate- and graduate-level religion and philosophy courses through these institutions.

One manifestation of this professionalization is a trend toward obtaining training that leads to an accredited degree, often from an institution outside China. China's cities have made possible advances in pastoral training by providing venues and serving as gathering points for students coming from various locations. Urban church leaders, both registered and unregistered, have played host to these students by organizing training opportunities, often involving instructors from other cities or from outside China. Although some of the more well-developed unregistered seminaries have been granting certificates to those who complete their studies, it is only within this decade that training centers, in cooperation with overseas educational institutions, began conferring degrees that are recognized abroad. Today it is increasingly common for urban church leaders in training to expect that the instruction they receive will lead to an accredited degree.

An experienced trainer who has worked for decades with both registered and unregistered pastors pointed out the benefits of accredited programs operating within China (as opposed to having students go abroad for studies). These include equipping leaders within their own contexts without making them relocate, and providing consistency in the level of training and the demands on the students. In addition, local congregations in collaboration with one another are able to fund the centers, thus reducing dependency upon outside resources.

CHANGING STATUS OF CHRISTIAN LEADERS

The trend toward professionalization changes the pastor's profile in the society. Whether among rural peasants or among Wenzhou's "boss Christians," leaders in the unregistered church have traditionally been bi-vocational, meaning that they held steady jobs while pastoring part time, and did not draw a salary from the church. In the case of the rural peasants, farming provided both a means to earn a living as well as the flexibility to spend more time doing church work during those periods when work on the farm was not so heavy. The Wenzhou "boss Christians" traditionally served as volunteers in the church while giving priority to running their businesses.[29]

With the older house church networks becoming more urban and with new urban congregations emerging, full-time pastors are becoming more common. This shift greatly increases the congregation's expectations of the pastor as well as the pressure on the congregation to provide for the pastor. Among unregistered urban professional congregations the fact that the pastor serves full time raises his status in the community. Even though many such pastors had formerly worked in education, business, or the professions before taking up full-time ministry, in their current positions their primary identity is pastor. Like their counterparts in the registered church, they are seen as professionals fulfilling a rather unique, but nonetheless legitimate, role in society. Their public presence vis-à-vis government, media, academia, and other social domains gives the church a voice in the society which it previously did not have. Even in Wenzhou, where churches have traditionally relied on volunteer leadership, more are now turning to full-time, formally trained pastors, and seminary programs have been launched locally to train such leaders.

The trend toward professionalization may not be entirely positive. While most Christians in China would welcome the enhanced skills and consistency that can come through pastors obtaining accredited degrees, some warn of a dangerous tendency toward emphasizing academic achievement over spiritual depth or character.

As one observer pointed out, leaders in the past were recognized on the basis of natural gifting, spiritual authority, and fruitfulness in ministry.[30] If these qualifications are superseded by academic achievement, the church may end up promoting within its ranks those who are gifted intellectu-

29. Ying et al., "Civic Communities," 90.

30. Y. R., interview with author, July 9, 2014.

ally but who are not necessarily prepared to serve. Another experienced overseas Chinese trainer who had also spent decades working with pastors in China reflected that, "Many church leaders, whether TSPM or house church, want degrees just to get the title. This is trendy . . . Knowledge is good if you get it step by step, but the gap between leaders and congregations becomes wider as the pastor learns more. Seminary training doesn't help you become a good pastor."[31]

The believer quoted at the beginning of this chapter, whose parents had been urban house church leaders, echoed these sentiments, expressing concern that an emphasis on professionalism could lead to pride, resulting in a church that has successful, well-executed programs but loses its fundamental spiritual character. Professionalism also widens the gap between clergy and laity, replacing the church's former collegiality with a new class system that differentiates between those with formal training and those without.

A PRE-DENOMINATIONAL CHURCH?

While traditional network leaders may have spoken approvingly of China's "post-denominational" church as evidence of the unity among believers in China, urban unregistered church leaders have been increasingly looking to existing denominational structures outside China to address issues of ordination, membership, and church management. An example of this trend toward denominational identity, which will be examined more thoroughly in chapter seven, is the tendency among many urban congregations, particularly those with connections outside China, to adopt the Reformed church tradition, the marks of which include a strong internal church structure with Presbyterian governance under a plurality of ordained elders who carry out ministry around the core devotions of scripture, the sacraments, and prayer, and who lead the church to carry out its God-given mission in the world.[32]

The "New Calvinism" currently popular in many urban church circles builds upon a strong Reformed orientation that has been present in China since the 1980s, due in large part to the influence of overseas Chinese Christian leaders including Jonathan Chao, founder of Chinese Church Research Centre and China Ministries International in Hong Kong, and

31. Otto Lui, interview with author, July 14, 2014.
32. Baugus, "Presbyterianism," 17.

Stephen Tong, an evangelist from Indonesia, as well as strong missionary and training efforts from South Korea. In more recent years the works of Reformed spokesmen including D.A. Carson, Timothy Keller, and John Piper have been translated into Chinese and have found fertile ground among China's urban Christians. Biblically and historically based, and logically presented, Reformed theology appeals to urban intellectual Christians who find within it a coherent system of thought. Its teaching on church polity answers the question of how the church should be led as it moves from a period of rapid expansion and fluid structure to a period of strengthening and consolidation.

A Reformed pastor in a second-tier city described his own theological transformation in the mid-2000s: "[W]hen you contrast the doctrines of the Reformed church and the teachings of the traditional church you will see a big discrepancy and you will feel a moment of sudden clarity. You will go from previously opposing theology to valuing theology, from no rationality to rationality, from a patriarchal system to a democratic system."[33]

Reformed teaching not only presents a comprehensive, systematic approach to the Bible and to issues of faith and church life, but its cultural and political implications also speak to the role of the church at a time when China's urban society is inviting Christian involvement. The concept of cultural mandate provides a biblical rationale for Christian activities outside the walls of the church, including in the realms of commerce, education, and government, where many urban believers conduct their daily lives. Similarly, the notion of cultural revival through the gospel (*wenhua jiduhua*) provides for a Christian response to the perennial question among Chinese intellectuals of how to revitalize Chinese culture in order to face the challenge of modernity.[34]

According to Andrew Kaiser, an American scholar living in China, much of urban Christians' discussions about Reformed theology are largely intellectual and are, in Kaiser's words, "more Weber than Calvin," driven by an interest in finding theological underpinnings for the church's engagement in society and involvement in political reform.[35] Fredrik Fällman observes, "The focus is more on Puritan teachings than on John Calvin himself. Such communities draw much interest from young urbanites, and they seem to

33. "Interview with a Reformed Church Pastor (2)."
34. Chow, "Public Theology," 152–68.
35. Andrew Kaiser, interview with the author, July 22, 2014.

attract these young people because of their solid stance on moral issues and their non-relative beliefs, contrasting with society at large."[36]

China's Reformed church leaders, on the other hand, see the contribution of the Reformed tradition as fundamentally spiritual. One large network of pastors reports that their concerted emphasis, through study and preaching, on the central Calvinist doctrine of God's grace for sinners has brought renewal to hundreds of congregations across China. Nevertheless, attempts to introduce a full-orbed Reformed denominational structure are meeting with resistance in some Chinese church quarters. While most church leaders would recognize the need to address the issues presented in the foregoing discussion—and would indeed acknowledge the potential contribution of Reformed tradition in these areas—not a few leaders caution against wholesale adoption of the Reformed "package," components of which have deep European or American roots and, in their opinion, are ill-suited to China's unique historical and cultural context.

This tension is particularly acute in areas of church life where Reformed practices run counter to traditional Chinese church culture. Concerning church governance, for example, while it is true that a new generation is developing a more collegial style of leadership, the accountability that comes with having a plurality of elders may still be threatening in a strong authoritarian culture where leadership requires maintaining "face" among one's peers. The Reformed requirement of male leadership runs counter to the reality in many, if not most, churches in China that (to paraphrase Mao) women hold up more than half the sky, shouldering the bulk of ministry responsibilities in congregations comprising more women than men. While some Reformed congregations now insist on male leadership as biblically mandated, other churches would find this requirement to be a significant stumbling block. Likewise, many Chinese churches find the practice of infant baptism foreign and may question its biblical basis.

A Shanghai pastor summed up the tension arising within the urban church as it wrestles with the question of denominational identity:

> In the process of establishing denominations, external liturgy is the easiest thing to imitate and internal culture is the hardest to assimilate since it comes from the unique provision and leading of God to a particular denomination in her history. Because of this, older traditional churches in China are often critical of new, younger, urban churches in their constitutionalization processes

36. Fällman, "Urge for Faith."

39

to establish denominations. It is very easy to import a denominational book of governance or church constitution or doctrinal catechism. Forming a proper governance model or church membership system is not a hard thing to do.

Though the establishment of a denomination seems like surface work, yet in its essence, it is work to establish Christ's Church. Therefore, in this significant process of constitutionalization, how can churches that intend to establish denominations not only inherit precious historic traditions, but also receive "new wine" in the gospel of Jesus Christ?[37]

PLACE, SPACE, AND FACE

The emerging urban church's shift from meeting in homes to meeting in semi-permanent public facilities has implications both for the form and function of the church itself and for its position in society. The term "house church" (*jiating jiaohui* or "family church" in Chinese) often conjures up images of a handful of believers, usually a family along with some relatives and neighbors, meeting clandestinely in the cramped sitting room of a sparsely furnished rural home or apartment. This might have been an accurate portrayal of the church during the Cultural Revolution, when all worship was forbidden and small family gatherings were the norm, as well as into the 1980s and 1990s when most believers were still found in the countryside and security concerns in the cities mitigated against any one house meeting becoming too large. The past decade, however, has seen a shift decidedly away from this traditional image and toward larger more public gatherings, a result both of the reality that apartments in urban China are not very spacious and of the growth of small fellowships, which may have grown out of campus or neighborhood Bible studies, that have become regular worship gatherings. A rising standard of living among urban believers, meanwhile, has made it possible for congregations to secure their own rented facilities.

While such meetings are still technically illegal, authorities for the most part appear to be taking a "wait and see" attitude toward these emerging urban congregations, perhaps out of the realization that it is easier to keep an eye on large groups that meet in the same place and at the same time each week than it is to keep track of dozens of smaller groups that may move from place to place. For the believers, a rented space provides

37. Wang, "New Wine."

the security of a buffer between their church attendance and their home life; should the church be raided by authorities, the individual members need not fear losing their own homes or personal property.[38] The stability of having a fixed location tends to promote the maturity of the church. One researcher noted that groups that had previously sat informally around a circle in someone's home, each one sharing as they discussed the Bible, were now sitting in rows, facing a podium and listening to a designated speaker giving a prepared sermon.[39]

NEW ECONOMIC REALITIES

Having fixed public locations for worship raises new economic considerations and is itself evidence of the new economic realities shaping the urban church. Although there exists great disparity between the financial resources available to an urban migrant congregation as opposed to one composed of middle-class professionals, the unregistered church in general is moving toward greater self-sufficiency. It relies far less upon donated resources from outside China and upon purely voluntary, often bi-vocational, leadership. Instead it is able to fund its own programs, including renting worship space, and to pay the salaries of full- or part-time staff. Urban Christians commonly pay for various types of training and seminars, from marriage conferences to seminary-level courses and even trips to the Holy Land. They are willing to purchase books and other resources, in contrast to a previous generation of Christians who believed that "if it is for ministry, then it should be free," and who relied on generous overseas donors for supplies of Bibles and training materials. The church's self-sufficiency removes the temptation that often accompanied surreptitious transfers of funds from donors outside China into the hands of a few believers (often including the pastor and a few close relatives or associates) responsible for their use.[40]

Nonetheless, the sheer volume of funds needed to sustain an urban unregistered congregation, particularly if it has paid staff, presents a host of new challenges. Since it cannot be registered as a legal entity it cannot have its own bank account. Trusted members must be relied upon to use personal or company accounts to keep the church funds. A committee of

38. C. C., interview with author, July 15, 2014.
39. Mary Ma, interview with author, August 15, 2014.
40. Otto Lui, interview with author, July 14, 2014.

members usually provides financial oversight, and in a congregation of urban professionals there are likely members with the requisite financial training to perform this function well, including reporting to the congregation about the church's use of funds. However, without any outside accountability (such as that which could potentially be provided through being part of a larger denomination, for example) the risk remains of a church leader or those who actually hold the money misdirecting funds for personal use.

Responsibility for holding the church's lease or deed, in the event the church decides to purchase its own facility, similarly falls to an individual congregation member or a business associated with the church. Where a business leader owns the property in which the congregation meets, such as is often the case in Wenzhou, this arrangement can be fairly straightforward. Still the question remains of what to do if this key individual were to leave the church, particularly if the departure were not on good terms. Similarly, if he or she were to pass away the congregation could be confronted by family members demanding custody of property or bank accounts in the name of the deceased.

As can often happen in charitable endeavors, those with the most financial resources tend to hold more sway over church matters. In the case of Wenzhou's "boss Christians," the relationship between wealth and influence in the church has been a part of the church culture. In newer urban professional congregations, where an increasing number of members may have considerable wealth, the stage is set for competing agendas, potentially putting the pastor in a position of arbiter between influential members and thus upending the church's traditional authority structure.

CULTURAL EXPECTATIONS

Finally, the trend toward fixed, visible locations for unregistered urban congregations fulfills a cultural need, giving the church "face" in the community. According to Dr. Kim-Kwong Chan of the Hong Kong Christian Council, "In China people look for a visible icon that represents the religious group. They want to see something tangible. Visibility is important for the church in a cultural sense."[41] Furthermore, in an age of "religious consumerism" the church must be able to compete for attention. Young urban professionals who spend their weekdays working in modern office towers and their weekends strolling through gaudy mega malls have come

41. Kim-Kwong Chan, interview with author, July 4, 2014.

to expect a certain level of comfort and sophistication. Traditional house churches meeting informally in crowded apartments do not appeal to this consumer mindset. For many young professional Chinese, the thought of being thrust into close quarters with a small crowd of strangers in somebody's home would be intimidating. In terms of accessibility, China's officially sanctioned churches under the TSPM obviously have the upper hand. Their large, prominently located facilities in major cities are generally packed on Sundays. In the minds of at least some church leaders, providing an equally welcoming venue requires that urban unregistered congregations rent or otherwise acquire space, usually in a commercial building, and outfit it in a manner consistent with urban Chinese expectations.

As of this writing, the epitome of such facilities would be Beijing's Zion Church, which occupies an entire floor of an office building in the north part of the city. Founded in 2006 by Pastor Ezra Jin, who formerly served under the TSPM at Beijing's Gangwashi Church, Zion Church boasts a worship hall that can seat 600. Entering the facility from the elevator lobby, visitors are welcomed by the church's mission statement displayed prominently by the front door. Next to the double-door entrance to the worship hall is a large cross, framed by Bible passages in Chinese and Korean. (Jin himself, like several other well-known urban pastors in China, is ethnically Korean.) Across the hallway is a bookstore and coffee bar, where patrons can order a latte to enjoy as they peruse their newest purchase in the adjacent seating area. Down the hall are the church's seminary library and classrooms, as well as nursery and Sunday school facilities. Pastor Jin himself has come under criticism from other pastors who are not comfortable with his high public profile. Although Zion Church may not be typical of China's urban congregations, most of which worship in more modest facilities, it does, however, represent a new standard to which at least some emerging congregations aspire.

REPOSITIONING THE CHURCH

The visibility of these church facilities may be seen as part of a larger effort to reposition the church in society. Whereas the traditional house church was hidden from society, and the registered church was prevented from playing a significant role in mainstream social or cultural life, a new generation of urban Christians desires to make the church visible. Doing so requires that the church shift its focus from being "otherworldly" to caring about and engaging with the concerns of society.

Shouwang Church in Beijing, whose vision is to be "a city built on a hilltop," typifies this decided shift. Not all urban Christian leaders would endorse Shouwang's overt public stance, particularly vis-à-vis the government. Nevertheless, Shouwang's pioneering role is widely recognized and has even been acknowledged in China's official media.[42] The church began public worship services when it brought together its ten home fellowships in 2005 and began renting space in an office building.[43] It has published its own periodical since 2007 and also has its own web site.[44] Its leaders have been outspoken about the need to be "on the surface" instead of "under the water," a stance which led them to engage in lengthy discussions with government officials over a period of years in an effort to gain legal recognition.

When those negotiations eventually failed, resulting in Shouwang losing its premises, its leaders resorted to holding worship services outdoors. On the morning of November 1, 2009, hundreds of congregants, along with robed choir members and musicians with their instruments, gathered in Beijing's Haidian Park in an unseasonably early snowstorm, much to the chagrin of passersby and police, who watched nervously but seemed uncertain as to how to respond. The congregation later moved into another rented facility, but when the landlord of that property was pressured into discontinuing the lease Shouwang again took to meeting outdoors. In a pastoral letter sent the night before Easter 2011, Pastor Jin Tianming, who was under house arrest, wrote, "The 'outdoor' in the outdoor worship is not a means to an end but a stand we are making before our Lord of glory and the authorities. It is a kind of worship before the only true God who is the only head of the church. And in this particular period of time, it is a worship that is even more precious than any hymn or sermon and would much more please God."[45]

THE CHURCH IN SOCIETY

The issue of positioning pertains not only to the physical presence of the church in the city; for some urban church leaders it involves making a

42. Liu Dong, "Estranged Brethren."
43. Hsu, "Beijing's Largest House Church."
44. Ying et al., "Civic Communities," 93–94.
45. Hsu, "Beijing's Largest House Church."

statement to the community and to the state about the church's rightful place in Chinese society. At a forum on religion in China held at Purdue University in May 2014, unregistered church leaders, scholars, and rights lawyers from China argued that the church's role is to lead the way in the fight for religious freedom by demonstrating to the public a non-violent civil disobedience movement. When enough people follow this example, the conference participants argued, then the government will have to recognize the legitimacy of religious freedom and public life. More than fifty participants signed the "Purdue Consensus on Religious Freedom," which called for freedom for Chinese "to practice their faith, to worship together, to establish religious venues, to use religious symbols, to publish religious books, and to disseminate religious faith."[46] Many leaders among China's urban migrant churches, on the other hand, see China's urban professional Christians as idealistic and—in the tradition of Chinese intellectuals—as having assumed the mantle of caretakers of society. These migrant church leaders instead assume a less confrontational stance, focusing on evangelism rather than consciously seeking to raise the church's public profile.[47]

Ying et al. contrast the "public theology" of Shouwang Church with this traditional view of the church's role, noting that migrant church teaching emphasizes raising the moral standard of believers and keeping family harmony. The focus is primarily inward.[48] It is true that China's Christians, having been raised in a Socialist society and inculcated with a community spirit, do participate in community activities, often as part of government-led campaigns. Nevertheless, the church has not been at the forefront in encouraging such activities. Yuan Hao, who is himself from a rural house church background, agrees that, while migrant believers may care for those in need within the church out of a sense of mercy, they still have a limited view of the world and their role in it.[49] Similarly Ying et al. observe that Wenzhou church members are primarily concerned about health and material prosperity, having a "utilitarian" mentality that sees God as being there to meet their needs and thus giving little time or energy to engage

46. Philips, "Beijing urged."
47. Yuan Hao, interview with author, July 22, 2014.
48. Ying et al., 87.
49. Yuan Hao, interview with author, July 22, 2014.

in outside ministry.[50] TSPM church engagement is limited due to political restraints, in what Ying et al. see as an example of "state-led civil society."[51]

In an article entitled "Raise the Cultural Level of the Church: Build a High Quality Church," one urban pastor gave this rationale for a repositioning of the church through social engagement:

> Community service is a major way for the church to leave its own walls and become a participant in society. Through this kind of service, the church can gradually learn how to communicate as an equal member of the community, thus becoming salt and light. Community service also allows the church to use a non-propaganda-centered method to live out the love of Christ through serving others, all while displaying the common ethics and values that Christians share with the rest of the world. A community-centered spirit is rooted in moral values, and the background of moral values is faith. Through community service that is rooted in their belief, Christians can both build church culture and live out a culture of love.[52]

Not all Christians in China (or outside China) would subscribe to this view that it is the role of the organized church itself to engage in community service. Some would make a distinction between the social involvements of Christians, either individually or in groups, and that of the church congregation as an entity. While China's urban Christians generally share the conviction that they as believers have an important role to play in society, how exactly to fulfill this role, and how far to go in carrying it out, remain topics of intense discussion. These questions will be examined further in chapter five.

50. Ying et al., 90.
51. Ying et al., 99–100.
52. "Building a Chinese Church Culture."

4

A Shifting Battleground

"For we do not wrestle against flesh and blood . . ."[1]

CHRISTIANS THROUGHOUT HISTORY HAVE seen themselves engaged in a battle that is ultimately spiritual in nature. Forces arrayed against them, political or otherwise, are physical manifestations of this unseen battle, which will ultimately consummate in Christ's return and reign. For a large part of the past century, China's Christians experienced this warfare as an ongoing conflict with a state that, if not intent on destroying the church altogether, was committed to limiting its size and influence. The battle lines were drawn between the church and those political entities (including, in the minds of many believers, the TSPM) charged with carrying out the Party's restrictive religious policy. These entities wielded a variety of weapons that included, at different times, personal coercion, intimidation, legal restrictions, harassment, imprisonment, and raw physical force. Fighting this battle required not only prayer and spiritual disciplines, but also a host of creative survival tactics. These tactics ranged from limited acquiescence or passive resistance to creating elaborate clandestine networks that enabled believers to advance the gospel message while keeping one step ahead of the law.

Today the nature of the battle has changed as the implementation of religious policy has shifted from aggressive control to the construction of a large box within which believers have a fair degree of space to maneuver

1. Ephesians 6:12.

as they carry out the work of the church. The enemy, still seen as ultimately spiritual, is now attacking in new ways as the benefits to the church that have accompanied urbanization—access to material resources, greater freedom of thought and expression, and new options for family life—form new battle lines defining the church's current spiritual conflict. The struggle is essentially a battle for the spiritual vitality and purity of the church over and against the forces of materialism, secularism, and moral decline. In the words of one pastor, "At present the main problem facing the church is not government persecution; in fact, this is unimportant to the church. No, the main problem is holiness. If the church is not holy, its witness is destroyed."[2]

REFRAMING RELIGIOUS POLICY

This shift can be traced back to 1982, when the Communist Party of China reframed its own struggle against religion in a document entitled "Concerning our Country's Basic Position on the Religious Question During the Socialist Period," otherwise known simply as "Document 19" (as it was the nineteenth Party document issued that year). Document 19 recognized that religion had not died out during three decades of Communist rule, nor would it be expected to die out any time soon. As China's focus shifted from rooting out hostile forces through class struggle to modernizing the country through economic development, religion went from being a "primary" to a "secondary" contradiction in society. The Party's aim thus shifted from eradicating religion to marshaling all available forces (including religious) within society to participate in the modernization effort. The Party's united front strategy would be to isolate and ultimately eliminate those religious elements that opposed Party rule while befriending and guiding those elements it deemed cooperative. As China has urbanized during the three decades following the appearance of Document 19, the Party has become increasingly less concerned about ideology and has focused instead on preserving social harmony. China's Christians are free to believe what they wish (as guaranteed in the revised 1982 Constitution), as long as they do not create or contribute toward instability in society. With the ascendancy of President Xi Jinping in 2012 there has come a renewed emphasis on ideology; however, as of this writing the emphasis remains on uniting religious believers in support of the Party's agenda rather than directly opposing religion.

2. "The Church Today."

Religious policy has thus become less a matter of controlling the specific activities of believers and more a matter of simply managing these activities. This management ideally takes place through the TSPM and its affiliated congregations and institutions, but, as most believers operate outside the TSPM umbrella, it can also be seen in the way in which local officials monitor unregistered church activities. Although direct attacks on some urban unregistered groups have taken place, the Party's *modus operandi* has generally been to let unregistered leaders know that they are being watched (often through periodic invitations to "drink tea" with agents of the local security bureau) and to warn them against becoming too large, having foreign contacts, or engaging in any activities that could be construed as political—all triggers that would likely invite more aggressive intervention by local officials.

THE CHANGING STATUS OF BELIEVERS

The shift in religious policy and implementation has been accompanied by a significant shift in the social status of China's Christians. No longer peasants, marginalized from the rest of society and secluded in rural areas, Christians are now increasingly visible as citizens in China's cities. The distinction is more than simply geographical; as urban citizens, China's Christians possess a degree of influence not previously enjoyed by Christians of past generations. This is particularly true of those in their forties and below who have college degrees and hold white collar jobs in business, government, or education—a segment that accounts for an increasing number of those found in the urban church.

With the prestige of a well-paying job comes a higher standard of living and the ability to contribute generously to the church. Unlike their rural predecessors, whose worldview was quite provincial, these believers tend to have a cosmopolitan outlook that allows them to view their Christianity in light of the larger social and cultural milieu. More sophisticated than their rural counterparts, they are less likely to be intimidated by, or to become targets of, corrupt local officials looking for an easy mark. A Chinese Christian friend once commented that in the rural house church, if the police came knocking at the front door, the believers would probably all disappear out the windows, but in the urban unregistered church the host would simply answer the door and say, "May I help you?"

GOD AND MAMMON

Increasing wealth among urban Christians has benefited the urban congregations in their ability to secure facilities, maintain programs, and hire staff. In a very positive way it has cut down on corruption and lessened unhealthy dependence upon the church outside China, as believers are now able to pay for their own training programs, books and other resources, and even educational opportunities overseas.[3] It has spawned new business opportunities through Christian publishing, seminars, counseling programs and other services. However, China's rising urban standard of living has also brought with it a rapidly growing materialism, seen by many pastors as the most serious threat to the church today. The transformation has happened quickly; in less than a generation the church has gone from being relatively impoverished, weak, and vulnerable to being increasingly well resourced. Church leaders consistently point to China's rampant consumerism—including a trend toward "religious consumerism"—and to the desire for wealth and status among young believers as presenting the most serious dangers to the future of the church.

Unlike in past decades, when being a Christian in China carried a huge personal price, today it is relatively easy, even fashionable in some circles, to be part of the church. The contexts may be worlds and generations apart, but the challenge facing China's church as it moves from being persecuted to being increasingly prosperous calls to mind the words of 18th century British reformer William Wilberforce:

> Christianity especially has always thriven under persecution. At such a season she has no lukewarm professors; no adherents concerning whom it is doubtful to what party they belong. The Christian is then reminded at every turn, that his Master's kingdom is not of this world. When all on earth wears a black and threatening aspect, he looks up to heaven for consolation; he learns practically to consider himself as a pilgrim and stranger. He then cleaves to fundamentals, and examines well his foundation, as at the hour of death. When Religion is in a state of external quiet and prosperity, the contrary of all this naturally takes place. The soldiers of the church militant then forget that they are in a state of warfare. Their ardor slackens, their zeal languishes. Like a colony long settled in a strange country, they are gradually assimilated in features, and

3. Otto Lui, interview with author, July 14, 2014.

demeanor, and language, to the native inhabitants, till at length almost every vestige of peculiarity dies away.[4]

Whereas a previous generation of Christians, primarily rural, experienced Christ in their poverty, urban church leaders today are concerned that China's urban Christians (not unlike Christians in other developed affluent societies) are in danger of being too materially satisfied to recognize their own spiritual hunger and too busy engaging in consumer activities to seek spiritual fulfillment. The Christian community in China has traditionally been loath to talk about money, considered an "unspiritual" topic. In a culture where, under Mao, most people were equally poor, this omission probably did not matter, as the topic would have been viewed as irrelevant. Today, however, in a culture awash with money, the lack of scriptural teaching on wealth has led some to embrace a prosperity gospel. Congregations erect large, sometimes ostentatious, structures because they have the means to do so and, according to some Christian leaders, because these visible signs of prosperity will cause nonbelievers to see the church as a "successful" institution.

Responding to a *Gospel Times* article on the high-profile demolition by local government officials of a large church structure in Wenzhou, one reader wrote, "The reason there are so many believers in Zhejiang is because of these big and beautiful church buildings. When outsiders see the good life of Christians, they are gradually drawn to the faith. If worship took place in secret, do you think there would be so many Christians in Wenzhou?"[5] With the highest Christian population of any Chinese city, Wenzhou has become famous for its many towering structures, some of which, resembling European-style cathedrals, are quite striking. In the words of one observer, because of the favorable social and political conditions, "Competition to build churches had almost become the order of the day. As soon as a new church was built, it was torn down and rebuilt again! Before the new building was even filled with people, they began to build an even bigger and more luxurious one . . . Many believers mistakenly think that tithing to support building a church building is the same as building a congregation. Since they believe this pleases God, they happily tithe to build a church building. Congregations often use church building projects as a means of uniting believers."[6]

4. Wilberforce, *A Practical View of Christianity*.
5. "Demolish!"
6. "Reborn from the Ashes."

A CALL FOR STEWARDSHIP

The current challenge would appear to be the development of a theology of stewardship that brings constructive meaning to abstract economic wealth, challenging both long-held traditional norms regarding the role of money in families and society, as well as the current culture of ostentation. Such a theology is necessary not only to address the use of wealth by individual Christians and within the church, but also the responsibility of Christians to the society at large.

China's yawning wealth gap directly affects the church. Although both the migrant worker and urban professional congregations are growing, anecdotal evidence suggests very little overlap or interaction between the two. Migrant pastors may desire to learn from their better-educated and better-resourced counterparts, but they often have no way to build a relationship with urban professional church leaders. Similarly, while leaders in the urban professional church might acknowledge their obligation to minister to the city's poor, geography, social space, and a lack of *guanxi*, or personal relationship, inhibit them from becoming directly involved in migrant communities. These pastors also face pressure from their members to improve services for the existing congregation, who might question why resources are being diverted to other groups outside the church.

While in earlier days China's Christians might have been united by a common social status and a common sense of dependence, both materially and spiritually, today urbanization and economic development have given rise to stark differences between various classes of believers. The danger to the urban professional congregations is that they become self-absorbed, existing as self-contained islands on the urban landscape but not growing beyond their current demographic. For the migrant worker churches, a lack of education and social experience within their ranks could perpetuate the cycle of poverty and keep them at subsistence level, particularly if migrant children are denied educational opportunities in the city and must either return to the countryside to finish their education (in which case most will drop out) or else, like their parents, settle for menial work in the city. These migrant worker offspring comprise potentially one of the most at-risk segments of the Christian community in China today. Swept up in the materialistic culture of the city, they desire a better life than that of their parents, yet, without role models, they have no clear road map for realizing that life, and their lack of education stands in the way of better jobs.

Class differences appear to be less stark in southern Chinese cities such as Shenzhen or Guangzhou, which have experienced large waves of rural migration over an extended period of time, leading to a greater degree of assimilation into the existing urban population (which, in the case of Shenzhen, was basically non-existent 30 years ago).[7] Whether other cities may follow suit in the future, producing more integration between urban professional Christians and upwardly mobile second- and third-generation migrant believers, remains to be seen.

IN THE MARKETPLACE OF BELIEF

The postmodern philosophy that all truth is relative characterizes the marketplace of belief that has opened up in China. With the relaxation of religious policy and enforcement during the past three decades, being a religious believer no longer constitutes a high-stakes commitment. In effect, one can believe anything as long as it does not precipitate action that the Party deems harmful to society or to its own interests. For China's Christians, when all truth is relative, it is difficult to preach the gospel as God's revealed, authoritative truth. Syncretism becomes common as those looking for a belief system pick and choose among various options, which may include Buddhism, Taoism, traditional folk practices, Confucian philosophy, elements of Christianity, or the teachings of a quasi-Christian cult. Against a backdrop of postmodernism, pastors struggle to nurture committed believers in an age of privatized faith, exacerbated by social norms that effectively separate one's convictions from one's behavior, particularly in the workplace. Church buildings are full, but pastors complain the congregants are merely "Sunday Christians," who profess Christ during church meetings but whose lives during the week demonstrate scant evidence of a Christian commitment. Commenting particularly on the marked increase in church attendance around Christmastime, two Chinese Christians writing in an online publication complained:

> Christians usually obey the Bible's instruction, "six days you shall labor, but on the seventh day you shall rest" (Ex. 34:21). So, every Sunday, they pick up the Bible which they have laid aside for a week, brush off the dust, and hurry off to church . . . As a result, it seems like Christians have an extremely respectful and joyous

---

7. C. C., interview with the author, July 15, 2014.

attitude toward the birth of Jesus. It also seems that there is a revival in the Church.

But crowded Sundays and exciting Christmases are a huge
contrast with the sparse numbers that usually show up for small
groups and other fellowship opportunities. Why are the small
group numbers so low? Why is it so difficult for the small groups,
places of such dynamic sharing, to attract those who enthusiasti-
cally attend church on Sundays? We need to think through this
issue; as a Christian, if you only busy yourself with things of the
world, if you indulge in the pleasures of this world, if you only go to
church on Sundays, how can you live an abundant Christian life?[8]

The result of this "Sunday Christian" phenomenon, the writers go on
to explain, is that Christians are not receiving regular spiritual nourishment
but instead come to "gorge" on Biblical teaching once a week, an unhealthy
practice resulting in uneven spiritual growth. They have neither an intimate
relationship with God nor an emotional attachment to the church. They
may suddenly draw close to God in an emergency, but even then they would
hardly know what to say, as they do not have a regular habit of prayer.[9]

RELIGIOUS CONSUMERISM

Postmodernism and the rise of the market economy have combined in urban China to create "religious consumerism," whereby believers choose experiences based on whether these meet their personal needs. In the general
populace this trend follows the pattern of picking a particular shrine or god
depending upon whether it will produce the desired result, be it business
success, good test scores, the ability to bear a child, or a satisfying dating
or marriage relationship. For China's Christians, "religious consumerism"
often consists of "church hopping," in search of a more interesting pastor,
better youth group or children's program, or even a more pleasant worship facility. In a sermon on threats facing the urban church, one pastor in
China stated,

One of the patent characteristics of post-modernity is a consumer
culture. Everything is consumed and consumable, whether it is
sacred or secular . . . "I consume, therefore I am." The value of
all things, people included, is validated only when consumed. The

8. "Sunday Christian."
9. Ibid.

Christian religion is no exception. Church attendees seek to use all that the church offers in order to satisfy their own wants and needs. Everything is liable to be taken advantage of, whether it's the preacher, the choir, the deacons, or even God himself. It is akin to being a church consumer: if the church doesn't satisfy one's appetite or meet one's goal, the consumer utters complaint, casts blame, and finds a new place to "go shopping."[10]

As a result, pastors lament that it is difficult to exert spiritual authority among believers, who are increasingly mistrustful of their pastors. Whereas rural church life was characterized by a spirit of sacrifice, many urban Christians view the church as a service provider and have come to have high expectations for what they will receive in return for their attendance and offerings. A Beijing pastor, reflecting on the implications of this trend for worship, warned, "Some look upon worship as a means of attracting those who are not yet believers, using music and songs to express their emotions. This diverts the worshiper's attention from God to his own feelings, with the result being that they may think that what is good and spiritual is merely expressing their inner thoughts and feelings."[11]

Growing individualism has caused the church to lose its family tradition and identity as a community of believers mutually committed to one another.[12] In the words of one young urban pastor, "The church is a social club (*julebu*). The pastor depends on exciting programs to keep people entertained . . . Believers expect God to bless them. They wouldn't know what to do if they encountered difficulty."[13]

Returning to William Wilberforce's observation, quoted earlier in this chapter, it may be argued that the past persecution did, in some ways, serve to strengthen the church. In today's urban environment the very factors that give the church new freedom and new opportunities could also bring about its decline. As one pastor told a foreign reporter who asked what would happen if the church were granted complete religious freedom: "We're finished (*jiu wanle*)!"[14]

10. Xing, "Five Major Challenges."
11. "Reflections on Worship."
12. J. H., interview with the author, July 22, 2014.
13. W. T., interview with the author, July 24, 2014.
14. "Cracks in the Atheist Edifice."

Along with post modernism and materialism, church leaders, like this pastor of an unregistered congregation in Beijing, cite rampant secularization as posing a serious threat to the church:

> One must not underestimate the influence of the secular zeitgeist on the church. Many in the church feel that the Bible's teaching is impractical and inapplicable, and that the way of the Lord and the way of the world are poles apart. They feel not that the Lord's way is simply hard, but impossible! Without the heart to serve and the resolve to follow in the way of the cross, how can one escape being secularized? Many go so far as to cut corners in church matters and do business according to secular principles . . . In society, churchgoers live according to its secular ways and set the sacred on the backburner. They are thus assimilated into society. Where is the witness of light and salt to be seen?[15]

An experienced trainer of pastors in China described the change in his students during the past two decades, particularly noting the growth of rationalism, driven by an evolutionary scientific mindset: "Culture is shaped by pragmatism and the survival of the fittest; everything needs to be effective. As a result theological training has to be pragmatic, fast." Compared to his mostly rural background students of 20 years ago, he sees this generation as having less of a spiritual mindset and less personal supernatural experience.[16]

THE BATTLE BEGINS AT HOME

Moral relativism and changing social mores have called into question traditional Chinese ideals of family life, while the effects of China's one-child policy and massive rural migration have significantly altered the structure and functioning of families, which have traditionally served as the core of Chinese social life. Many urban pastors see believers' ability to meet these challenges and to realize the biblical ideal for marriage and family relationships as critical to the church's effectiveness. One commentator writing in the online journal *Church China* warned, "God takes great delight when we build up the family, while the devil's work is to break up the family . . . In China the crisis of marriage and family is becoming clearer and clearer."[17]

15. Pinghuang, "Five Major Challenges."
16. L. D., interview with the author, July 7, 2014.
17. "The Church Today."

A new generation of urban Christians, unfamiliar with biblical teaching on the family, struggles to reconcile its faith with the realities of the urban Chinese social environment. At the same time, urbanization and a higher standard of living for many have brought unprecedented options for families, particularly in the area of children's education, but with these options have come intense pressure and difficult choices. As China "grows old before it grows rich," the question of who will care for its burgeoning elderly population looms large for young families and for the church. Thus, for many Christians faced with difficult personal moral choices, relationship conflicts, and decisions about priorities, the spiritual battle starts at home.

CHRISTIAN MARRIAGE

China's urban Christians, many of them relatively new believers, find themselves torn between biblical teaching about relationships and the social pressure to find a mate. The Bible clearly instructs that believers are to remain sexually pure before marriage, and that the marriage relationship is not merely an economic arrangement or a means of finding personal fulfillment, but a spiritual union with Christ as the head. For many Chinese Christian women, the tension is exacerbated by the relatively high ratio of women to men in Chinese churches, posing the dilemma of whether it is better to marry a nonbeliever or to remain single.

Responding to a popular article from the official Chinese news agency, *Xinhua,* which asked, "Are Chinese Men Good Enough for Chinese Women," the Christian intellectual online publication *Territory* asked, "Chinese Men and Women: Who, in the End, is Good Enough for Whom?"[18] [19] The original article, based on surveys of urban single Chinese women, took Chinese men to task for being generally unkempt and lacking in social graces, and took Chinese women to task for not caring about men's appearance but instead emphasizing wealth and security in their choice of a partner. In contrast to the *Xinhua* article's assertion that, "The relationship between the two sexes is originally supposed to be one about mutual pleasure," the *Territory* writer lamented, "Acknowledging the mutual attraction between the two sexes and expecting mutual support for each other has been reduced to a joke, not to mention the self-sacrifice and real practice of submission

18. "Are Chinese Men?"
19. "Do Chinese Men and Women?"

to another's character necessary to preserve a loving marriage." He then proceeded to address the spiritual condition of both sexes:

> In God's view, we all lack the glory and honor with which we originally lived. The fact of the matter is that men and women hurling eggs and insults at each other demonstrates our brokenness . . . This world tells men that only those who are strong, tough, smart, and in control can survive, succeed, and "deserve" a beautiful woman. This is similar to one sick patient using his own twisted behavior to cater to the morbid psychological needs of another sick patient. Jesus Christ, through His life and teachings, tells us that mankind's greatest weakness is actually his greatest strength. The love between these sick people seems promising, but actually it is because we learn how to depend on Him as our healer that we no longer depend on our own wisdom.[20]

Both men and women who have been created in God's image, the article concludes, have the same problem, in that this image has been marred by sin and can only be restored through the divine work of Christ. Acknowledging their own brokenness and their dependence upon Christ will thus enable men and women to mutually respect one another.

The church has responded in practical terms, firstly, through teaching on the biblical basis for relationships. Addressing the consequences of sexual sin, a *Christian Times* article mentioned the loss of trust with one's partner, loss of respect for oneself and for the other person, the impact on one's marriage in the future, and, finally, God's judgment. The article concluded with the exhortation, "Very few people will want to marry someone who has already been sexually active. Wisdom clearly instructs us not to live in such a way."[21] For those not yet married, a half dozen or more Christian dating sites provide opportunities for Christian singles to meet one another. Several of these sites offer marriage counseling or referrals to counseling resources and other services. As with similar sites outside China, users are advised to be cautious in establishing relationships online. A caveat on the dating web site *Jesus Free Wind* gives these helpful reminders: "Online dating is still somewhat risky. Be sure to verify the true faith, personal information, and condition of the other person. Protect yourself against fraud by meeting only at churches or other public places."[22]

20. "Do Chinese Men and Women?"
21. "Single Christians and Love."
22. "Chinese Christian Dating Sites."

For those already married, urban congregations provide marriage retreats, often with the assistance of overseas Chinese organizations that specialize in this area. Pastor Zhou Ming of Olive Tree Church, an unregistered congregation in Beijing, sees marriage ministry as foundational: "The church needs to increase the level of importance it places on guarding marriages. The true meaning and significance of marriage must be taught in the churches: one husband and one wife, one man and one woman, for your whole life. There are all kinds of problems in society, but whatever kind of social problem there is, you need stable marriages to be the foundation." Zhou adds that marriage retreats are also important because they provide emotional support for husbands and wives who are often tempted to give up on their marriages.[23]

Perhaps the greatest difference between Christian and non-Christian couples is the faith that difficulties in their marriages can be worked out, and that they personally can change to become better spouses and parents. Caroline Huang, an educator and author of a book on parenting published in China, contrasts this belief in the possibility of change with the traditional concept of fate, which she sees at work in many marriages. Women whose husbands are unfaithful, for example, may simply resign themselves to their misfortune. Whereas non-Christians might attribute a spouse's personal characteristics to his or her genes or blood type, Christian couples acknowledge the need to take personal responsibility for one's character and behavior, believing that the Holy Spirit can bring about change.[24]

TRAIN UP A CHILD

The single-child phenomenon has raised the stakes in parenting, as the hopes not only of the parents but also grandparents, aunts, and uncles are pinned on the only child. The pressure parents feel to make their child a success prompts urban parents to invest heavily in toys, books, and extracurricular tutoring. Many of the current generation, however, forfeit the task altogether, resulting in a large number of children being raised by grandparents. Parents who were themselves only children may find that they are not ready for parenting or, because of work or social responsibilities, are too busy. Many urban migrant families send children back to the countryside to be raised by their grandparents, because both spouses are

---

23. "Why Marriage Retreats."

24. Caroline Huang, interview with the author, July 16, 2014.

working and thus do not have time to take care of the children, and because the children can attend school in their home village or town, where they still have their *hukou*.

For Christian parents both extremes—either "over-parenting" or abdicating their parental responsibilities—present a dilemma as they seek to follow the biblical injunction to bring up their children "in the training and admonition of the Lord."[25] Spending all available time and financial resources on the child while neglecting their marriage relationship can create a false sense of entitlement on the part of the child and result in problems in the marriage later on. The tension between church involvement and family responsibilities can become acute as parents try to balance the social and family pressure to focus on their child with the expectation that they remain active in church activities. On the other extreme, delegating their parenting responsibilities to their own parents, who may not be Christians, significantly reduces their opportunities to be involved in their child's spiritual development, increasing the likelihood that, although they themselves may be committed believers, their child may not follow in their footsteps.

Urban congregations, both registered and unregistered, are responding to the needs of children by offering Sunday school programs and, in some cases, youth groups and family camps. Child-rearing classes for parents and grandparents are also popular. Although government policy during the 1980s and 1990s often forbade children from taking part in religious activities, these local restrictions have eased in most places, making it possible for churches to engage in children's work.

CHINA'S EDUCATIONAL DILEMMA

The primary focus of parents' attention is on their child's education. A rising standard of living has created unprecedented educational opportunities; competition to get one's child into a better school is fierce. Yet with the target still being a high score on the national college entrance examination, education at all levels consists mainly of preparation for taking tests, leaving little time for a student's spiritual, physical, or social development. China's centuries-old test-taking culture promotes educational attainment as an accomplishment in and of itself. Unfortunately, unlike in Imperial China or even during the time of China's opening up under Deng Xiaoping, there is today no automatic correlation between getting a degree and finding one's

25. Ephesians 6:4.

place in society, not to mention making a meaningful economic or social contribution. Meanwhile, competition for places at the best schools—from kindergarten on up—becomes stiffer as more middle class families enter the ranks of those who can afford educational choice for their one child.

As a result of this test-taking culture, students are ill prepared for the real-world challenges they will face after graduation. Disgruntled with what many see as a dead-end educational street, more and more families are seeking alternatives outside the state-endorsed educational sector. These alternatives include homeschooling (including starting homeschool cooperatives), semi-legal private schools, programmed learning such as the ACE (Accelerated Christian Education) curriculum, or sending children abroad for high school or even earlier. The expense involved in pursuing the latter approach puts immense pressure on single children, as evidenced by this comment by a student headed abroad for study, "I don't want to go overseas to study because I know my family is going to spend all their money on my education. What if I don't meet their expectations?"[26] For Christian families the challenge is made more complex by their desire to inculcate their children with a Christian worldview, which runs counter to the prevailing values of the state education system. Some Christian intellectuals would go so far as to say that education is the most important field for Christians in China to pursue, as providing an alternative to the state-sponsored atheistic curriculum is essential to equipping a new generation of Christian leaders who are firmly rooted in a biblical worldview and who can thus impact their culture.

Professor Li (a pseudonym),[27] a Christian sociologist at a university in southern China who researches secondary education, believes that a biblical philosophy of education is needed in order to counter both the prevailing atheistic paradigm as well as the deeper underlying Confucian ethic that informs education, not only in China, but in other Asian societies as well. According to Li, this ethic in China has reached an extreme, as achieving a degree (or degrees) and the prestige that this brings has become the terminal goal of education. "The whole purpose of education is to get into university," he says, "but when students get into university they don't study. They don't have any goals. As a result they don't know what to do with themselves."[28] Little attention is paid to the innate talents or inter-

26. Caroline Huang, interview with the author, July 16, 2014.
27. Li Dong, interview with the author, October 29, 2013.
28. Ibid.

ests of students, and little thought is given to what they will do following graduation. Is it any wonder, he asks rhetorically, that many students end up disillusioned after graduation or find themselves in careers which are personally unfulfilling?

According to Professor Li, this trend may be observed generally among Chinese around the world; however, in China it is more extreme because there is no real civil society, only the state. Unlike in other countries, where social contributions are valued along with academic achievement, in China there is neither the motivation nor the room for social participation; hence the only way to validate one's accomplishments is through test scores.[29] This system runs counter to the biblical view of education, built on the premise that all persons are created in the image of God, with unique gifts and talents to be developed in order that they might live for his glory. The Christian paradigm of education, says Li, should be about developing students in all areas, not simply academic, in preparation for a life of service, as opposed to elevating one's status by earning a degree or attaining a prestigious position.[30]

EDUCATIONAL ALTERNATIVES

Christians looking for an alternative are enlarging the space of private education—but at great risk and without a clear road ahead. These alternatives fall into two main categories. One approach is to pursue Christian education with an openly biblical curriculum, either informally through some form of homeschooling cooperative or by starting a church-based school. Both are technically illegal, although in the latter arrangement some legal cover may be sought by registering as a business or through a cooperative relationship with a sympathetic public school nearby. The other approach is to launch a fully licensed private school that fulfills state requirements but is staffed by Christian faculty and administration. Although following the state-mandated curriculum, such a school can seek to promote a Christian worldview through the way in which various subjects are taught and through character training and extracurricular activities. Activities for parents, such as marriage or parenting seminars, provide additional ways to inculcate Christian values.

29. Ibid.
30. Ibid.

The former model is currently the most widespread. Anecdotal evidence suggests there are a few thousand such schools in operation around China. These schools are generally limited by a lack of qualified teachers and adequate facilities. As with many unregistered church congregations, these schools frequently need to relocate as they do not have permanent sites. For curriculum they often depend upon a system of programmed instruction translated from materials developed overseas. Several home-school curricula developed by Christians in the United States have found a sizeable market in China. At least one popular program offers an accredited high school degree in the United States upon completion, which ostensibly would then allow a student to apply to university abroad. In reality, however, this certification provides no guarantee of university admission.

Critics point out that this programmed instruction aligns very closely with the traditional Chinese model of education, relying on individual study and rote memorization, and, unless supplemented by other activities, is not helpful in promoting the development of social or creative thinking skills. Some church-based schools in smaller cities have gotten quite innovative. One pastor who started his own school using programmed instruction also teaches the students music and media production skills, assigns them community work projects, and organizes sports competitions with youth from other Christian groups nearby.

Although church-run kindergartens may be popular with young Christian families, enrollment drops off after first grade, when parents become concerned about the quality of the education and their children's educational future should they remain outside the state-run system. One study of urban church-based schools found the majority of students were either children who had not been able to succeed in public school or were offspring of migrant workers.[31]

For Christian-run private schools that are legally registered and accredited, the most formidable obstacle appears to be finding and retaining adequate facilities. In order to achieve accreditation they must demonstrate that they are equipped for a full range of school activities, requiring science labs, athletic tracks, and other amenities. With land at a premium, satisfying this requirement becomes a stiff challenge requiring a sizeable financial investment. This funding may come from an investor who sees the school as a good business proposition but who may not wholeheartedly support its Christian purpose. In many cases the ownership of the property may not

31. Cheng, "China's Christian Education Today."

be clear, as when a Christian-run school takes over the facilities of an existing private or public school that, for whatever reason, is no longer able to function. Where schools have been able to succeed in attracting a sizeable number of students and making the operation financially viable, their success then can become a liability, as investors or local cadres attempt to take over the school through reclaiming the property or through legal maneuvers. Gaining the requisite permissions to launch a school in the first place is a daunting and costly process, usually requiring good relationships with a host of officials from various government departments. Recruiting suitable faculty who have the academic background, teaching skills, and Christian commitment needed to fulfill the combined educational and spiritual mission of the school is also difficult.

The biggest obstacle facing both models is the uncertainty that parents and students must face regarding the students' education in high school and beyond. Once students disengage from the state education system they have little to no chance of sitting for the *gaokao*, or university entrance examination, and thus no hope of attending university in China. For families who can afford it, the alternative is to send their children abroad for high school, usually to the United States, in preparation for attending university abroad. A number of Christian schools in the United States are happy to oblige, both out of a desire to serve families—especially Christian families—in China, and because of the financial boost to their schools brought about by the influx of Chinese students. Some schools abroad have already formed collaborative relationships with private schools in China, allowing students to earn credit while still in the country in preparation for the transition to study overseas.

The vast majority of Christian families in China, however, are unable to make this investment. For these families, pursuing Christian education for their children in China is fraught with risk and uncertainty. Many head down this path in hopes that China will have reformed its education system by the time their children reach high school age. According to Caroline Huang, reform will likely come about incrementally as China's education authorities allow universities to experiment with alternatives to the *gaokao* in their student recruitment.[32] Substantial education reform does not appear to be on the horizon currently. Given the growing dissatisfaction both with the current system and with the results it is producing, however, it is likely that during the next decade China's leaders will see the need to make

32. Caroline Huang, interview with author, July 16, 2014.

major changes. If, and when, that should occur, China's Christians will be eager to play a role.

CHINA GROWS OLDER

A final concern facing Chinese Christian families is the care of older parents, grandparents, and other relatives. As China's elderly population mushrooms and its working-age population shrinks, families find themselves caught in the middle of this demographic divide. Cultural expectations and legal requirements put the onus on them to care for older family members, but neither the government nor the society at large are currently prepared to provide the resources needed to support this effort. Furthermore, the Bible is clear that taking care of one's own family is a primary responsibility of believers: "But if anyone does not provide for his relatives, and especially for members of his household, he has denied the faith and is worse than an unbeliever."[33]

For many Christian congregations in China, the immediate concern, especially in the rural areas, is caring for elderly pastors in their later years of life. TSPM-affiliated churches have the advantage of owning property that, in some cases, can be used to develop a home for the elderly that is adjoining or adjacent to the church. Several have already taken this step, and others may be expected to follow suit. Younger urban pastors are faced with caring for parents who, in many cases, still live in the countryside or in smaller cities. Many of their congregants find themselves in a similar situation. With living space limited in the city, it may not be practical or desirable to have older relatives move in with the family. While they might want to personally offer care out of a sense of filial piety, the reality is that many will need to look for third-party solutions.

Looking further across the society, two possible large-scale responses emerge, both of which provide opportunities for China's urban Christians not only to care for the elderly in their midst but also to offer a service to the larger community, thus enhancing the church's standing in society. Given the right mix of expertise and investment, along with a favorable regulatory environment, urban Christians could potentially play a leading role in both areas. One response involves training home health workers to visit seniors who are still living on their own or whose family is not able to care for their

---

33. 1 Timothy 5:8.

needs. So far this appears to be the government's favored approach to elder care as it is seen as more cost-effective.

The other response is to construct residential care facilities. Investors in this space have thus far targeted the high-end market, where income from wealthy clients and their families will more than cover the cost of providing first-class services. The biggest need is among middle- and low-income clients and their families.[34] Preferential treatment and incentives, including tax exemption and waived or lowered administrative fees, are available for companies wanting to invest in this area.[35] Both approaches require training skilled and non-skilled workers. Given the overall lack of expertise nationwide in gerontology and other related fields, however, the means of training these workers is not readily available in country.

China's church, like most entities in society, is struggling as it grapples with the challenge of China's ageing population. On the other hand, the Christian community in China is the one entity that does have access to a sizeable pool of potential personnel, both professionals whose expertise could be applied specifically to senior care, as well as unskilled workers who could be trained for support roles. With a biblical ethic of caring for others, these Christians could bring to their service a motivation that would not be found among others who see senior care as simply a business opportunity. If they were able to create a viable model, it would likely catch the attention of government officials who have been tasked with finding ways to care for the elderly and who have resources at their disposal to do so, but who are wary of committing funds without first seeing firsthand that the proposed solution is going to succeed.

Several small-scale projects are currently being undertaken by individual church congregations and by Christian entrepreneurs and healthcare professionals, some in collaboration with Christians outside China. Thus an urgent concern facing urban Christian families in China—how to care for ageing relatives amidst widespread social change that has left traditional practices unworkable—has created an opportunity for China's Christians to exercise their beliefs and values in practical ways. Doing so would gain the church legitimacy within society as Christians are seen caring not only for their own needs but also for the needs of their community. The following chapter explores this theme further by examining the relationship between the urban church's witness and social engagement.

34. Shobert, "Senior Care."
35. Yao, "Golden Years."

5

Into the Light

"Let your light so shine . . ."[1]

FOLLOWING A STIMULATING DISCUSSION over tea, the professor sitting across the coffee table in a hotel lobby carefully moved the empty cups to one side, leaving a large empty space in the middle. He had been discussing the state of the church and its role in Chinese society. The key to the church's future, he said, was how it understood this role.

"Here is where the church is." He pointed to the cups at the end of the table. "It is on the fringes of society, so consumed with its own issues that it does not recognize the huge empty space in the center of society."[2]

That empty space, representing the lack of a common system of belief and the lack of trust that is so prevalent in China, is waiting to be filled by something, said the professor. If the church were to rise to the occasion and fill this space, it would be recognized as truly having something to offer society.

AWAY FROM THE MARGINS

In the past decade the church in China has begun its move from the margins of society toward the center. Many would trace the beginnings of the

1. Matthew 5:16.
2. Conversation with author, June 28, 2012.

church's journey away from the margins to May 2008, when the Wenchuan earthquake in Sichuan province galvanized a groundswell of volunteer activity unprecedented in recent Chinese history. Among those who responded were Christians from more than 15 cities across China. The year 2008 is commonly referred to as the dawn of volunteerism in China; Christians in China would point to 2008 as the year that the church moved off the sidelines and onto the stage of social engagement.

According to Dr. Huang Lei, an orthopedic surgeon from Wuhan who coordinated Christian relief efforts in 2008, preparation ahead of time by urban church leaders resulted in their ability to respond quickly and on a scale never before seen among Christians in China. Dr. Huang and his wife became Christians in 2003 after a friend who was visiting from abroad shared the gospel. Unable to locate a church nearby, they started a Bible study in their home, which grew to 100 attendees in four months. To accommodate what had by then become a functioning church congregation, they began meeting in rented office space.[3] In the days following the disaster, as relief supplies and volunteers poured in from across China, Dr. Huang founded China Christian Love Action (CCLA), a quasi non-profit organization that would eventually establish offices in three cities in China.

Dr. Huang's organization would ultimately be responsible for setting up thousands of tents for emergency shelters, dozens of tent schools, and more than ten community centers. During the rebuilding phase CCLA volunteers stayed on, focusing their attention on providing trauma counseling and caring for orphaned children. According to official accounts of the relief effort, more than 60 percent of volunteers who came to Sichuan following the quake were Christians, and it was the Christians who remained in the area longest to assist in the rebuilding effort.[4]

Reflecting on the church's experience in 2008 and again in 2010, when CCLA took the lead in mobilizing the Christian response to the Yuxu earthquake in Qinghai province, Dr. Huang noted that the relief and rebuilding work had been undergirded by a strong network of unregistered urban congregations across China whose close cooperation enabled the mobilization of funds and personnel. According to Huang, although these congregations have yet to be recognized as legitimate by the government, yet, in the eyes of the common people, they have already gained recognition. The Sichuan experience represented a turning point for the church

3. Moll, "Great Leap Forward," 23.
4. Huang, "Beautiful Testimony," 12–15.

and its relationship to the larger society. It has also become a touch point for Christian leaders today as they proclaim what they see as the church's cultural mandate. In the words of Huang, "Now is the time for the Chinese church to enter into, meld with, influence, and renew the society."[5]

A TURNING POINT

Social service is one way in which the church is seeking to engage with the society. Commerce is another area, with Christian business leaders actively seeking to apply biblical principles in a sphere known to be rife with unethical practices. With the marketization of publishing and the rise of online activity in China have come new opportunities for Christians to enter the media space. On university campuses and in academic forums across China and internationally, Christian intellectuals are bringing a faith perspective to scholarly discussions on China's current moral state and future direction. Finally, some Christians are engaging in direct advocacy or political action in an effort to expand the social space for Christian activity in China.

The movement of Chinese Christians into these various arenas has been significant. At the same time, it should be noted that not all urban believers are of the same mind concerning the church's social involvement, with some holding to the position that the church as an organization should not undertake direct social action, although believers in the church may choose to do so, either individually or in groups. In this regard, China's urban Christians are "crossing the river by feeling the stones," (to quote a Chinese idiom popularized by the late reformist leader Deng Xiaoping), seeking to live out their Christian commitment in ways that are both faithful to Scripture and relevant to the society in which they live.

A CRISIS OF FAITH

The notion of social renewal is a common theme among urban Christian leaders as they consider what it means for the church to take its place in mainstream society. In an article entitled "The Achilles' Heel of China's Rise: Belief," Liu Peng, a researcher in the Chinese Academy of Social Sciences and founder of a Beijing-based think tank on religious policy, writes

5. Ibid., 13–15.

that China's current "crisis of faith" is the result of more than three decades of rapid economic development divorced from any underlying ideology. Absent a common belief system, Deng Xiaoping's dictum, "To get rich is glorious," remains the guiding principle in society. Public trust is at an all-time low, scandals are uncovered at increasingly higher levels within the government (leaving the public to speculate on what *hasn't* yet been uncovered) and corruption and fraud are rampant across all sectors of society. In Liu's words, "The reason why Chinese society has seen an abundance of outrageous and ridiculous phenomena, with little corresponding uprightness, is not because we are short of money. Rather, it is because we have lost our faith . . . While the core of the value and belief systems that buoyed the Chinese spirit in the past has been destroyed, we have not yet made the innovations necessary to develop and maintain a new core value and belief systems for contemporary Chinese."[6]

Although the official ideology of Marxism, Leninism, and Mao Zedong Thought has ostensibly remained dominant through China's decades of reform and opening, and although most people in society would at least give lip service to these tenets, yet in reality, says Liu, the Chinese today have no shared system of belief. This is the "elephant in the room" that, according to Liu, stands in the way of China's future development. While China continues to experience a downturn in social morality, Liu laments that "Our media rarely faces these questions directly or comes straight to the point: why is it that the core values and belief system that the authorities repeatedly propagate do not work? Do the Chinese, who have simply solved the problems of food and clothing, in fact hold any value or belief system? What exactly went wrong with the faith of the Chinese?"[7]

Liu is not necessarily referring to religious faith. Faith, for Liu, is simply a set of beliefs one internalizes, which provides meaning and motivation for life. In the case of a nation, "Faith is necessary to offer a fundamental reason for its existence and development and to motivate its citizens to work together for greater achievements."[8] This faith is comprised of the common goals of its citizens. The faith of the individual and of the nation are thus connected. In China's current "crisis of faith," this connection has disappeared. Liu draws a parallel with Republican China, in which the Kuomintang's Three Principles of the People were held up as the guid-

6. P. Liu, "Achilles' Heel."
7. Ibid.
8. Ibid.

ing principles of the nation yet remained empty slogans for the majority of China's people. Under Mao the idea of continuous class struggle, perpetuated through serial political campaigns, provided the ongoing spiritual connection between the people and the state. The religious fervor attached to this class struggle reached a boiling point during the Cultural Revolution, which Mao launched in 1966, and was finally spent by the time of his death ten years later.

With Deng Xiaoping's ascendency to power in 1978 the people's attention turned to economic development, and the promise of building a better life, both personally and as a nation, replaced class struggle as the common object of faith. However, Liu contends, this "worshipping a golden calf" does not provide moral or spiritual support. On the contrary, unbridled pursuit of profit has resulted in widespread corruption, environmental degradation, and a realization among the newly wealthy that being rich does not equate to having a meaningful life. In Liu's words, "China is once again faced with the question of 'what do we believe in?'"[9]

THE CHURCH ON DISPLAY

China's urban Christian leaders believe that engaging with their society is essential to the credibility of the church's witness. Asked what concerned them most about the future of the church in China, two leaders of a Chinese Christian online media organization both replied that the church ought to be more socially involved. Chinese intellectuals have expectations of the church, they explained, yet when these intellectuals visit actual church gatherings they are often disappointed. The institution that they assume ought to be taking a more active role is instead too occupied with its own immediate needs to get involved. If these scholars saw the church behaving differently, their estimation of the church and of Christianity would change accordingly. Similarly, speaking of churches affiliated with the TSPM, Rev. Dr. Kim-Kwong Chan, General Secretary of the Hong Kong Christian Council, said the way to achieve political legitimacy is to provide services to the society.[10]

Unlike in past decades, when the church had a much less public presence and the gospel message was conveyed primarily through clandestine small group meetings or personal relationships, today's urban church is on

9. P. Liu, "Achilles Heel."

10. Kim-Kwong Chan, interview with the author, July 4, 2014.

display through the presence of believers in business, education, government, and other areas. Sociologists Li Ma and Jin Li, drawing on their three-year ethnographic study of Christians in two major cities, note that "their active presence in the public space and their more explicit expressions of faith is [sic] helping to diffuse Christian values into civic discourse and to provide an alternative to the official ideology. Secondly, these elite-led Protestant groups have also oriented the unregistered churches on an organizational level towards more openness and more active social engagement."[11]

The desire of urban church leaders to respond to the social dilemmas described above grows not only out of their own theological convictions and sense of cultural mandate, but is also rooted in the realization that, for the society to take the church seriously, the church must be seen as caring about those issues that are of concern to society. To paraphrase the professor who was quoted at the beginning of this chapter, the open space created by the lack of a coherent ideology has been generally acknowledged, and China's urban citizens are watching to see who will come forward to fill it. He and others like him believe that, if the church can play this role, it will be seen as relevant. Stepping into this arena thus brings social as well as political legitimacy. It also moves Christianity from being, in the minds of many, a foreign and somewhat suspect belief system, to being seen as more "Chinese" as it provides indigenous solutions to indigenous problems. Finally, urban Christian leaders see engagement with society as essential for keeping the church from becoming too inwardly focused.

For Pastor Ezra Jin of Zion Church in Beijing, the obvious moral decline in society raises the question of the church's role; hence, answering this question is critical for the church's future witness. In the words of Jin,

> In the past twenty years, the economy has experienced significant changes, including breathtaking economic growth, but many problems have emerged; morality has declined and there is spiritual emptiness . . . some say that relationships between people are growing increasingly superficial, causing society as a whole to become increasingly indifferent. Organized religion over the past twenty years also seems to have experienced significant growth. It appears to be flourishing, however, it still has absolutely no ability to influence society, let alone improve society. In fact, internally, there is much corruption within organized religion. We need to be aware that in a rapidly transforming society like the one in which

11. Ma and Li, "Remaking the Civic Space," 12–13.

we are living, it is necessary to consider how to use love, truth and the gifts granted us to serve society and those in need."[12]

THE EXTENDED FAMILY

Zhou Ming, a retired physician and pastor of an unregistered congregation in a suburb north of Beijing, sees families within the church as the starting point for a credible witness to the community. "If our family wants to influence another family," Zhou says, "as a Christian family we should get along well and love each other, and the light that shines forth from our family will attract them."[13] According to Zhou, by blessing the community, the church demonstrates that it cares not merely about spreading the gospel message but also seeks to have a positive social impact.

Gerda Wielander contrasts the Christian idea of love for one's neighbor with Chinese sociologist Fei Xiaotong's notion that, in Chinese society, love radiates outward in concentric circles, beginning with one's immediate family and moving in diminishing amounts away from oneself and toward one's more distant relatives, friends, and others within one's relationship network. Outside of that network one has no connection to people in the society at large and hence no obligation to care for their welfare. In Christian community, on the other hand, "brothers and sisters" may be found among any who come into the church, regardless of their social status or previous relationship. This duty to love others comes from an externally imposed moral code that is not dependent upon the status of the individual. These new "kinship ties" substitute for what is otherwise missing in fragmented urban society, where one can no longer rely on centuries-old relationship networks for support, and thus lend social legitimacy to the role of the church in the city.[14]

Pastor Jin puts it in spiritual terms when he says, "We ourselves not only need to receive God's salvation and blessing, but we also need to rely on God's love, grace, and blessing in order to assume responsibility for and to love the society in which we live, and enable those around us to gain a foretaste of the Kingdom of Heaven."[15]

12. Jin, "Social Responsibility."
13. "Beijing Pastor."
14. Wielander, *Christian Values*, 34–39.
15. Jin, "Social Responsibility.

CULTURALLY BOYCOTTED

Liu Peng sees the church's engagement with the larger society as key to its continued contextualization as a truly Chinese religion. Yet, as an article on urban mission posted on a popular Chinese Christian website pointed out, the church is still ambivalent toward the society, and vice-versa. "Although currently maturing, Christianity in China is still not prepared to greet a fresh, new China; at the same time, society as a whole also has not formulated a necessary response to the rise of Christianity."[16] Amidst a culture in which popular thought is still largely informed by Confucian tradition, Christianity is not given public recognition. "Culturally boycotted" in popular society and in intellectual circles, Christianity is still viewed largely as a Western religion and has yet to move from a "suspect" to a "neutral" position in society.[17] According to sociologist Mary Ma, "Culturally speaking, to the modern Chinese, Christianity has always been an alien culture, a representation of Western-ness. So to convert to Christianity means turning away from one's Chinese roots."[18]

Historian Lian Xi is not optimistic about the church's role as a significant contributor to China's future cultural development. Drawing on his study of indigenous Christian movements in the first half of the 20th century, Xi points to what he sees as the church's tendency to absorb, rather than to replace, traditional folk practices. Xi views Christianity as primarily appealing to the masses and as shunning political activism, thus alienating itself from those seeking spiritual inspiration for social change. Xi writes,

> As in the case of popular religious movements in pre-modern China, which were usually unable to complete their intellectual formulation and to find legitimate political or social expression, contemporary popular Christianity has been condemned to a similarly stunted political growth. Persecuted by the state, fractured by its own sectarianism, and diminished by its contempt for formal education (theological or otherwise), it will probably also remain, as sectarian religious groups did in the past, in the state of intellectual decapitation."[19]

16. "Future of China."
17. Huo, "Two Transformations."
18. Ma and Li, "Remaking the Civic Space," 14–15.
19. Xi, *Redeemed by Fire*, 242.

Others, such as Huo Shui, the Chinese intellectual quoted in chapter three, are more hopeful about Christianity's prospects as a cultural contributor: "If Christianity can come out in time with a position as the provider of social ethics and morals and provide a spiritual belief system for Chinese society, if it can address the loss of faith of the Chinese people, then the people, the society, the culture, and China's rulers will completely change their opinion of Christianity."[20]

GREAT EXPECTATIONS

Finally, China's urban Christian leaders view the church's social involvement as critical to the healthy development of the church itself. Without such engagement the church could easily turn inward, becoming preoccupied with its own internal needs and thus losing its very reason for existence. Citing the recent decline of Christianity in Korea, Pastor Jin exhorted his congregation,

> God has great expectations for us. He expects his people to live out his plan and to be an acceptable witness . . . The leaders of the Korean church have discovered that during the past several decades the church has been concerned only with individual salvation and ignored the needs of society; has placed value only on individual blessing, and neglected its mission to society; has only emphasized church growth, and ignored societal responsibility; has only cared about the next life and disregarded this present life . . ."[21]

Andrew Kaiser, an American scholar living in China, remarks that young urban Christians in China, in contrast to Christians of previous generations, do not feel constrained to privatize their faith, but rather expect that their Christianity should impact every area of their lives. However, the lack of role models, says Kaiser, makes it hard to know what form this should take. Hence the popularity of the few openly Christian celebrities whose micro blogs provide examples of how Christians can make a contribution to their society. For Kaiser, how to live out their faith in a holistic way is the major question facing today's urban believers.[22] In the eyes of sociologist Mary Ma this is already beginning to happen: "Comparatively

20. Huo, "Two Transformations."
21. Jin, "Social Responsibility."
22. Andrew Kaiser, interview with the author, July 22, 2014.

speaking, the emerging Protestant groups have become agents of change in all walks of life amidst an otherwise stagnant political scene . . . [M]any educated believing journalists, actors, lawyers, and businessmen are making their religious convictions known in all areas of public life. Their faith compels them to do things differently than what the post-Communist state requires, and their independent actions are attracting increasing attention from the public."[23]

GOOD WORKS

As recounted at the beginning of this chapter, 2008 was a watershed year for Christian social involvement. In the ensuing years, Christians have emerged as a significant force in China's growing charity sector. Addressing the question of how China's Christians are having an impact on their society, Gerda Wielander concludes that this sector is the primary area where Christian ethics and values are most prominently lived out. Wielander adds, however, that, due to the government's unwillingness to make space for Christians in the charity sector, most efforts are often small-scale, under-resourced, and lacking in professional expertise.[24] The official restrictions that limit the growth of Christian-run nonprofit organizations include the unregistered church's lack of legal status and hence lack of a legal platform on which to build nonprofit work, the inability to openly utilize religious symbols, lack of access to public media, and a general mistrust on the part of the government and on the part of others in the nonprofit sector. Most successful nonprofit work in China requires cooperation with the government, which many unregistered Christian groups are unable to pursue. Even if a Christian-run organization is able to reach sufficient scale to warrant seeking registration with the Ministry of Civil Affairs, it would not likely be granted.[25]

These restrictions are exacerbated by a general lack of legislative support for the nonprofit sector. Although acknowledging the importance of the sector for China's continued social development, officials have nonetheless been loath to provide the legal framework and legal guarantees that would allow this sector to flourish, choosing instead to keep most charity work within the realm of government-organized non-government

23. Ma and Li, "Remaking the Civic Space," 14.

24. Wielander, *Christian Values*, 155.

25. Ibid., 80–81.

organizations, or GONGOs.[26] Despite decades of economic reform China is still structured along Leninist lines. Every organization must serve some political purpose, and authority must at some point come back to the Party. The growth of the GONGO sector, while giving some appearance of civil society, has effectively kept social organizations under the thumb of the Party. In areas such as education, where the Party maintains a firm national agenda, the space for nonprofit involvement is tightly circumscribed. Furthermore, the regime has been unwilling to allow the majority of China's registered NGOs to raise funds from the public. Doling out government funds selectively to groups it endorses enables the Party to direct their activities toward government priorities while isolating other NGOs whose agendas it may find threatening.

Creating a level playing field for NGOs in China would require acknowledging the legitimate role that Christians play in society. So far the regime has not been willing to take this step. In the case of Huang Lei, the nonprofit pioneer introduced at the beginning of this chapter, his organization never received official registration although it had government contracts to do charity work in Sichuan and, at the height of its operations, had some 200 church congregations involved. The group eventually disbanded. As of this writing Huang Lei is back in his hometown of Wuhan, where he runs a food pantry out of his church in cooperation with the local government.

The church's dilemma, says Rob Gifford, former China editor for *The Economist*, is that "Christianity is a bottom-up faith; China is a top-down country."[27] Given the current restrictions on formal nonprofit activities, many Christians like Huang Lei are resorting to more low-key approaches involving informal collaboration with government officials. An unregistered pastor in eastern China encourages local congregations to identify one need within the community and then to talk to local officials about how the church can help.[28] Another rural background believer now living in the city says that, while some Christian leaders may be called to be pioneers in openly promoting social change, every church can have a role in legally serving its local community, for example, by providing tutoring for children from migrant families. He advises that the church congregation first have a well-defined goal and be clear about its own calling, then

26. "Enter the Chinese NGO."
27. Rob Gifford, conversation with author, June 7, 2014.
28. L. J., interview with author, January 22, 2014.

mobilize members to form a team and begin putting down roots through its service to the community. In this way, he says, people will experience the love and spirit of sacrifice of Christ.[29]

BEYOND THE PROTESTANT ETHIC

Wenzhou's "boss Christians," as described by Cao Nanlai and others,[30] are entrepreneurs who have one foot in their businesses and the other in the church. Using their status and material resources as means to build up local churches, these men function both as bosses and pastors in a church culture where, until recently, trained full-time pastors were the exception rather than the rule. These "boss Christians" present a somewhat colorful and, one could argue, somewhat extreme, example of a much wider phenomenon, namely, that of Chinese Christian business leaders.

A wealth of anecdotal evidence suggests that many of these came to faith following a personal crisis, often related in some way to their work. The successful manager of a watch factory in southern China, for example, met with both marital and financial problems as a result of a downturn in business. Left with almost nothing, he accepted a friend's invitation to attend a meeting of Christian entrepreneurs. There he heard the gospel message and eventually made a decision to follow Christ. In the months that followed, his marriage was restored and he was able to restart his failed company, gradually rebuilding to the point where, not only was the factory successful, but he was also able to open a restaurant.

For many business leaders, their conversion is accompanied by the stark realization that they can no longer continue conducting business as usual now that they are Christians. They come to see practices common in the Chinese business community, such as tax evasion, dealing in counterfeit goods, giving and taking bribes, and frequenting nightclubs as a means of entertaining clients or officials, as violating the commands of Scripture. An article on Christian entrepreneurs in *Global Times*, the English-language arm of the Party mouthpiece *People's Daily*, tells the story of one such individual, the head of a drug company, whose sales plummeted after he stopped helping his hospital customers evade taxes by issuing false receipts.

---

29. Yuan Hao, interview with author, July 22, 2014.

30. Cao, *Constructing China's Jerusalem.*

His sales staff resigned, and others in the industry shunned him for breaking the unwritten rules of the trade.[31]

BUSINESS FELLOWSHIPS

Like many others, this particular entrepreneur found support in a business fellowship, of which there are probably hundreds in cities across China. The fellowship plays an evangelistic function, introducing non-believers to the faith. Since there are usually more women than men in China's churches, the business fellowships, which tend to be overwhelmingly male, offer a safe environment for men to share mutual struggles and to explore spiritual matters. For new believers, the fellowship is a place where they can become grounded in their faith. As many of the issues they face in the business world are not issues that normally come up on Sunday mornings, the fellowship provides a venue for learning from more experienced peers how to deal with these common challenges. As one expatriate Christian CEO put it, "The theological truths are pretty simple; knowing how to put them into practice gets complicated."[32] As a bottom line, fellowships require members to agree that they will not evade taxes, take bribes, or keep mistresses. Some fellowships provide specific training in character, ethics, or leadership, often involving a more experienced business leader from another city or from overseas as the trainer.

The fellowship can also provide a staging area for direct involvement in addressing social issues. Fellowships in Wenzhou are well known for raising funds among their members to contribute to needs within the community. In Shenyang, a fellowship led by a successful restaurateur requires members to tithe, with the money going toward relief projects or evangelistic work among China's ethnic minorities. For the Christian community at large, the fellowship may provide a broader function of enabling cross-pollination of ideas and building of relationships between church congregations that might otherwise remain rather isolated from one another. While making these positive contributions, many business fellowships nonetheless remain weak, as there is currently no national-level network to link them together (and doing so could be seen as a threat by Chinese officials who are wary of any social groups forming inter-city ties). Given the hectic

31. Chen, "Between God and Mammon."
32. Michael Barbalas, interview with author, June 29, 2014.

work and travel schedules of business leaders, it is also difficult to maintain consistency among participants in the fellowships.

PUTTING FAITH TO WORK

While the expectation is that Christians should somehow conduct business differently, the question of what exactly this should look like remains a difficult one. On an individual level, Christian business leaders are expected to give up ungodly practices that are prevalent in the secular business world, to adopt a higher ethical standard, and to share the gospel personally with others. Taking one's faith into the corporation is more challenging, but interesting models are beginning to emerge. The expatriate business leader quoted above spoke specifically of the need to start with the values of the company and then to see that those values are extended throughout the enterprise. Over and against what he sees as the prevailing Confucian view of employees having value only to the extent that they contribute to the firm's bottom line, he seeks to demonstrate respect for all within the company. He also seeks to counter the traditional reliance on *guanxi*, or personal relationships, to determine who receives promotions or other benefits, by promoting an ethic of fairness.

The restaurant business is one field in which Christians are seeking to have an intentional impact. The watch factory owner mentioned above opened a seafood restaurant together with a former nightclub owner who had given up his previous business when he became a Christian. After their chef was converted, he decided to stop adding MSG to his dishes out of concern for their customers. Their supplier is another believer who operates a fish farm in a neighboring town. Before this man became a Christian his ponds became infected and the fish died. Later, as a Christian, he felt called to nurture fish that were healthy. He eventually found a specialist who taught him how to put herbal medicine into the ponds. In return for supplying fish to the restaurant, he requires that the waiters at the restaurant explain where the fish are raised, including the fact that, in accordance with biblical teaching, the blood is removed before the fish is cooked, resulting in a fish that is safer and more nutritious.[33] Given the prevalence of food scandals in China since the mid 2000s, a supply chain that ensures the safety and quality of the food produced becomes itself a source of value. Such "Christian value chains" may in the future become more common in

33. Y. R., interview with author, July 9, 2014.

other sectors and may even become a competitive advantage as believing CEOs explore the connection between their faith and their businesses.

Dr. Angel Lu, a China-born comparative literature scholar now living in Hong Kong, suggests that Christian business leaders in China and elsewhere can go further in making this connection. While Christian business leaders and some academics are eager to celebrate the phenomenon of hard-working Christian CEOs as the embodiment of the Protestant work ethic, Lu believes that the Christian's calling in regard to economic and business undertakings is, according to the Bible, way beyond the model and level of Protestant ethics. In his well-known study, Max Weber, who made an oft-quoted connection between Protestant ethics and capitalism, was actually critical of both. According to Lu, the superficial, or perhaps intentional, misreading of Weber has served its historical function—in China, it helped to spur interest in Christian faith as people recognized the role that this faith played in the economic prosperity of capitalist countries.

As the Christian population in China has grown larger and more mature, and as Western Christians have become increasingly alarmed about the ills of capitalism, Lu suggests it is time to search for a solid, Bible-based theology concerning the economic implications of Christianity. Matters that have long been taken for granted, such as the accumulation of wealth, the profit motive, and inalienable property rights, may all need to be rethought from a biblical point of view. "In short," Lu says, "Christians can do much better than just being more excellent in the workplace or being more moral than non-believers. They can and should aspire to the Biblical definition of our roles—stewards in the economy of God."[34]

THE POWER OF THE WORD

Up until recently it was not possible for Christians to engage the larger society through media, since print and broadcast outlets in China remain under the control of the Party and off-limits to religious groups. This situation has improved during the past decade through changes in the publishing industry and the explosive growth of the Chinese Internet. China has 663 state-owned publishers, all of which are required to work within the shifting censorship parameters set by the Party. In the pre- and early-Reform eras when publishing was largely state-subsidized, these publishers produced mostly textbooks and books for political purposes. With economic

34. Angel Lu, interview with the author, October 31, 2014.

reform has come the need for these publishers to become self-sustaining. As a result the state publishing sector is recognizing the role of some 10,000 private publishing services companies, which work with authors to develop books and then contract with the publishing houses to get them into print, as a means of enabling the publishers to become profitable. The rising education levels and increasing disposable incomes of China's emerging middle class, meanwhile, have created a new market for books.[35]

Into this new publishing environment have stepped young, college-educated Christians, many of whom have studied overseas or have at least been exposed to a range of literature from outside China, and who have seen the opportunity to translate and publish some of these works in China. Christian authors and publishers outside China, eager to enter the China market and to promote the availability of Christian literature in China, have joined in the effort by giving rights to their books and helping to subsidize publishing projects. (In more than a few cases, unauthorized translations of popular Christian books have appeared in China, sometimes in multiple versions.) Publishing services companies, some run by Christians, serve as middlemen in the process, working with authors to contextualize their books (and sometimes to tone down overtly Christian content) and with censors in an effort to make sure they will be able to obtain an ISBN number for the book. As of this writing well over a thousand Christian titles, 80–90 percent of which originated outside of China, have gone through this process and are on sale at a few hundred Christian bookstores in major cities as well as through online outlets, including Amazon and the popular e-commerce site Taobao.

Although the growth in the Christian book market has been significant, given that only a handful of titles, mostly academic in nature, had been available on the market up until the early 2000s, the economic model remains problematic. Despite the additional distribution made possible by the likes of Amazon, profit margins are extremely narrow. Given the relatively limited demand, publishers are not willing to print in large quantities. As in other markets outside China, most Christian bookstores operate at a loss and need to supplement book sales by offering giftware or other products, or by receiving subsidies from a church or other entity. The few indigenous authors who could potentially make it into print cannot afford to spend their time writing, as cash advances are generally not available and

35. Gary Hopwood, interview with the author, July 2, 2014.

royalties are slim if not altogether nonexistent. They are also too occupied with their academic, business, or church responsibilities to be able to write.

Publishing options made available through the Internet address some of these economic concerns and open up new channels for Christians both to convey their message publicly and to organize for greater social involvement. China is second only to the United States in the arena of self-publishing, which has become a recognized channel for budding novelists to deliver their works to the reading public. Once the readership grows to a certain level these authors can charge for their works. Several are earning considerable incomes simply by virtue of the number of people purchasing their works online. As long as it is the author distributing his or her own work, an ISBN number is not needed.[36]

CHINA'S ONLINE CHRISTIAN COMMUNITY

Although Christian writers have yet to achieve this level of recognition online, the overall amount of Christian activity on the Internet within China is significant. Thousands of web sites deliver Christian news, sermons, worship music, dating services, and a variety of virtual training courses—including full seminary courses offered by recognized theological institutions overseas. Among the most visited sites are *Gospel Times* and *Christian Times,* two online daily periodicals covering news of, respectively, the official church under the TSPM and the unregistered church. Similar sites cater to intellectuals, pastors, Christian business leaders, and other audiences. Individual congregations, such as Dr. Wang Yi's unregistered Early Rain Reformed Church in Chengdu, have their own sites, as do the China Christian Council and many churches associated with the TSPM. Joann Pittman, who directs the *Chinese Church Voices* project,[37] writes, "The reality is that there is a thriving Christian community online where believers are participating in conversations about what is going on in China and the world, discussing issues and engaging in debates, accessing theological training, offering encouragement and doing evangelism."[38]

36. Ibid.

37. *Chinese Church Voices* (http://www.chinasource.org/resource-library/chinese-church-voices/) provides English translations of articles, sermons, blog posts and other online writings of Christians in China.

38. Pittman, "China's Online Christian Community."

This Christian content is largely unregulated. Pittman makes the point that the four most well-known providers of Christian content on the Internet all have their IP licenses on their home pages, indicating they are in compliance with relevant regulations and have registered with the appropriate authorities.[39] Provided content does not stray into politics or present views on current events that are contrary to the official line, Christians are generally free to post what they wish. Some site managers tell of learning where the boundaries lie, largely through trial and error. As there are no clear guidelines to refer to, they must rely on their own judgment to discern what is appropriate. They know they have crossed a line when they receive a phone call from the Internet authorities telling them that a certain post needs to be removed. Over time they get a sense of what is or is not allowed, although these parameters continue to shift along with the political winds in China. A particular topic, source, or even region of the country or world that is completely innocuous one day may suddenly become politically sensitive.

The conversation is even more far reaching on the micro-blogs written by believers or within the ever multiplying chat groups on WeChat or QQ, two popular social media platforms in China. As of 2012, nearly 90 percent of China's more than 500 million Internet users were active on micro-blogs.[40] Among the most popular Christian micro-bloggers is the well-known actress Yang Xin. Her posts have covered such topics as the connection between faith and character, how she seeks to live out biblical principles in the acting world, and her relationship with her husband, who is also a Christian. Responses to questions from fans include quotations from the Bible and examples of how she applies these truths in her life.[41] Other popular Christian micro-bloggers include radio personalities, authors, musicians, and business leaders, including property tycoon Pan Shiyi, with more than 17 million followers. *Zanmeishi*, a worship music micro-blog, has more than 360,000 users who have registered to receive three 140-character messages per day. A family-oriented micro-blog has more than 17,000 registered followers.[42]

The scope of China's Christian Internet presence and the benefits it brings to the Christian community, both in terms of access to information and resources as well as its ability to connect believers across the country,

39. Ibid.
40. Hornemann, "Weibo."
41. "Testimony of a Christian Artist."
42. Gary Hopwood, interview with the author, July 2, 2014.

are significant. Through the online witness of the well-known bloggers mentioned above, non-Christians are being exposed to a Christian world-view. The social impact of China's online Christian presence remains to be seen, however. By its nature the Internet creates communities of users. With hundreds of millions of users and a huge amount and variety of content, it forces users to decide with whom they will interact and which content they will consume. In this sense the Internet takes the concept of "nar-rowcasting" (the antithesis of broadcasting) to its extreme; niche markets for any kind of content or any kind of personal interaction can be created as long as the demand exists. China's Christian online community is no exception. Multiple sub-communities are beginning to proliferate based on theological persuasion, denominational affiliation, occupation, gender, age, or interest. The more specialized these groups become, the less likely they are to appeal to users outside the Christian community.[43]

FROM THE CLASSROOM TO THE COURTROOM

The growth of Christianity among China's intellectuals during the past 25 years is arguably unprecedented in Chinese history. Out of a generation of activists who filled Tiananmen Square in 1989 emerged a number of Christian leaders, including many who operate from outside China but who nonetheless exercise considerable influence. In addition, the "cultural Christian" phenomenon pioneered by Liu Xiaofeng in the 1980s gave birth to Christian study centers on campuses around China and to a wave of re-search and publishing on the contributions of Christianity to the develop-ment of Western culture and possible implications for China's own future.

Today a new generation of younger Christian scholars combines a strong personal faith with a desire to integrate that faith into their academic endeavors. For many this translates into active efforts to apply Christian principles to social issues through low-key lobbying for legal reform, em-ploying academic forums to speak out publicly, and, in the case of human rights lawyers, coming to the defense of those whose rights are being im-pinged upon by the state. China's new urban churches are a catalyst for community among these Christian intellectuals, some of whom serve a dual role as pastors of individual congregations and leaders among their peers through writing, speaking, and participating in conferences. Unlike the previous generation of "Cultural Christians," whose voice was heard

43. W. E., interview with the author, July 13, 2014.

primarily within the confines of the academy, the current generation is engaging society across multiple sectors not only through intellectual inquiry and discussion but also through action, made possible in part through their use of the Internet and their involvement in international networks.

Liu Xiaofeng, who received his ThD from the University of Basel in 1993 and went on to serve as Academic Director and Senior Research Fellow at the Institute of Sino-Christian Studies in Hong Kong, was emblematic of a generation of scholars that emerged in the 1980s to break new ground in the study of Christianity's impact on Western culture. Although professing an affinity with and appreciation for Christianity, Liu and others like him did not necessarily make a personal faith commitment. Few identified publicly with a particular church, perhaps in part because doing so could jeopardize their academic positions. Out of their explorations emerged a new genre of scholarly works, gathered under the rubric of "Sino-Christian Theology," consisting mainly of translated Western texts and reflections on them, along with new journals exploring historical, sociological, and theological themes. Christian study centers, eventually numbering more than 30, began to appear in university philosophy and religion departments on campuses around China.

The "cultural Christians" found support from overseas organizations including the Institute of Sino-Christian Studies in Hong Kong and, later, the Center on Religion and Chinese Society at Purdue University, which helped to underwrite conferences and publications and which provided stipends for advanced studies outside China. These scholars introduced Christianity as an historical phenomenon and cultural resource but did not address specific contemporary social or political concerns. One exception was the Christian sociologist He Guanghu, who signed Chapter '08, a document authored by dissident Nobel laureate Liu Xiaobo calling for significant political reform, and who later became more open about his own Christian faith. According to Fredrik Fällman, these "Cultural Christians," who showed "how faith was possible in post-Mao China," have in recent years lost influence, as a new generation of Christian intellectuals has emerged to play a different kind of role.[44]

The growing stature of this new generation may be seen in its prominent role in drafting the "Oxford Consensus," a document emerging from a symposium convened at Oxford University in 2013. The sixth in a series of annual Chinese theology symposia organized by Wang Wenfeng,

44 Fällman, "Urge for Faith."

a Wenzhou Christian who studied theology in Singapore, the symposium was unique in that it drew not only Christian intellectuals but also scholars representing the Liberal, New Confucian, and New Left schools. Although individual Christian scholars had interacted with their counterparts from these schools in previous conferences, this was the first time Christians were given equal footing along with the other groups, suggesting the perceived legitimacy of the public intellectuals within their ranks.[45] Participants included not only scholars but also government officials, artists, and members of the media.[46] The prominent role of Christian scholars in this gathering was particularly significant given fundamental differences between the Confucian and Christian traditions and the desire of some in the Confucian camp to paint Christianity as a "foreign religion" that has no role to play in an era when China is rediscovering its own glorious traditions.

The perennial question in the ongoing Confucian/Christian dialog concerns the innate nature and perfectibility (or lack thereof) of humankind. As Gerda Wielander points out, Chinese Christian intellectuals argue that the logical conclusion of Confucianism is tyranny, as it mistakenly assumes the inherent goodness of persons and results in elevation of human leaders and dependence on human wisdom, instead of acknowledging the limits of human wisdom and the need for the transcendent.[47] Nevertheless, Yang Fenggang of Purdue University's Center on Religion and Society in China sees hope for further cooperation between the two groups: "At present, Confucianism is not a civil religion, but it could be. In that case, however, it has to take Christianity into consideration. Together, we can contribute to building a new civil religion which is not only for China but also for the larger world. Some Confucian fundamentalists treat Christianity as a competitor, but that is not necessary."[48]

The document emerging from this symposium encapsulated the areas on which all could agree, namely, the need for pluralism, fairness, and justice within Chinese society as the nation moves ahead in its pursuit of the "China Dream." While affirming their love for China, participants nonetheless pointed out the conspicuous social problems that have accompanied China's rise to prominence. Reaching back into history, they asserted their traditional role as intellectuals to be the "critics and sentinels of society"

45. Johnson, "Oxford Consensus."
46. Swells, "Tyranny of History."
47. Wielander, *Christian Values*, 114–15.
48. Doyle, "Confucian Comeback."

and the transmitters of China's cultural heritage to the next generation. They insisted that political power derives from the people and the purpose of government is to serve the people's interests. As China continues its rise they urged that it promote peaceful coexistence and that international disputes be solved in a manner that is mutually beneficial to China and other nations.[49]

As intellectuals of various philosophical and political persuasions seek to be heard, it is significant that in this symposium the different schools chose to put aside individual agendas and conscientiously worked at agreeing upon a set of basic principles, thus strengthening their collective voice toward a state that could otherwise dismiss them as scattered and inconsequential. Given the historical inability of Chinese intellectuals to yield to one another's opinions and work together with those who do not share their point of view, the specific role that Christian intellectuals played in bringing about this consensus, including the actual convening of the symposium, and whether Chinese Christian intellectuals might be expected to play more of a mediating role among intellectuals in the future, merit further investigation.[50]

This current generation of intellectuals, rather than looking at Christianity as merely an historical or cultural phenomenon, is concerned with its role in contemporary society. For individual scholars this inquiry entails research into how Christian principles may be applied specifically to particular academic disciplines. One anthropologist in Shanghai points out that scholars of his generation tend to have had a more systematic education, most having had the opportunity to study overseas, and are thus better equipped than their predecessors to excel in their given disciplines while developing a Christian understanding of their respective fields. For him it is not a matter of imposing a Christian paradigm but of creating the space for alternative views to be entertained. In his own field he seeks to challenge traditional views of religion, not negating social or political perspectives but at the same time making a case for the legitimacy of the experiences of individual believers. This professor finds that his colleagues are not satisfied with the state of current research and are open to new possibilities. The biggest struggle, as he sees it, is maintaining a sense of a higher calling amidst an academic culture that emphasizes producing papers in order to get published or to get projects funded by the state. Many Christian scholars,

49. "Full Text."
50. Wielander, *Christian Values,* 128.

he says, simply lack the time to integrate their faith and their profession, allowing them to present an integrated view to the Christian community and to the public.[51]

Other Christian scholars seek a more public forum in which to engage directly with social or political issues. Liu Peng, a professor in the Chinese Academy of Social Sciences, launched the Pu Shi Institute for Social Sciences in the 1990s for the purpose of exploring China's religious policy and advocating for reform. His conferences and web site have featured scholars from around the world dealing with issues such as the role of religion in the market economy, comparative religious laws, the nature of China's unregistered churches, the implementation and consequences of China's current religious policy, and specific proposals for new religious legislation.[52]

A VOICE FOR JUSTICE

Finally, there are those Christian intellectuals whose faith leads them to participate in the legal arena, undertake advocacy, or venture direct political action. On the individual level, believers may take to the Internet to speak out against perceived injustices in society. Following the announcement last year that 300 million abortions had been performed in China since 1971, a pastor wrote in the online journal *Kuanye* an article entitled "Another Baby Slaughtered; Where is God?" He began by recounting a recent carjacking incident in northeastern China in which the thief, upon discovering that an eight-month-old boy had been left in the back seat, strangled the child and hid his body in the snow. The writer compared this tragedy, which had sparked outrage across China, with a similar incident in the United States in which the thief abandoned the vehicle he had stolen and called the police after discovering a baby girl, also eight months old, inside. The vehicle was recovered and the girl was rescued unharmed.

Asking "Why did the American thief abandon the car and spare the life of the baby while the Chinese thief did not?" the article then turned to China's family planning policy for the answer: by telling society that it is okay to take the life of unborn children for the sake of the country's economic development, this policy has cheapened the value of life to the point that the car thief did not think twice about strangling a child in order to complete his crime. Citing two other well-publicized cases of abuse related

51. J. H., interview with the author, July 22, 2014.
52. "The Institute."

to China's family planning policy, the author closed by saying these events "should serve as reminders to Chinese people that we have to stand against the evil one and say, 'No!'"[53]

Such criticism of government policy entails significant personal risk, and most pastors would not venture to be so outspoken online. On the church level, likewise, politically active congregations are more the exception than the rule. Some, however, may take up causes within society or may seek to defend their right to exist and to worship openly. Gerda Wielander points out the political education function played by the publications and web sites of congregations such as Wang Yi's Early Rain Church in Chengdu and Fangzhou Church in Beijing. Through these means, as well as through messages from the pulpit, believers are being sensitized to social and political issues and mobilized to take action.[54]

Beijing's Shouwang Church earned international recognition on Easter Sunday in 2011 when it was forced from its rented premises and began holding outdoor services. According to church leaders this confrontation resulted from years of negotiations with city officials about registering the church as a legal entity. In the end the negotiations proved futile, since the officials were not prepared to allow the church to register without coming under the auspices of the Three Self Patriotic Movement.[55]

Ezra Jin of Zion Church in Beijing, a strong proponent of unregistered churches "going public," sees the Chinese house church movement as a type of non-violent civil disobedience and potentially the largest civil rights movement in China. While holding up the example of Shouwang as a church that has been willing to be on the frontline of the unregistered church's struggle for legal recognition, Jin nonetheless cautions Christians against only looking out for their own rights and neglecting rights abuses occurring outside the Christian community. Jin and others expect that the church's defense of its own rights will lead the way for greater freedom of association, speech, and assembly within the larger society.[56]

China's Christian human rights lawyers echo the conviction that Christians need to be concerned about the rights of those outside the church. While these lawyers have taken on high-profile church cases, they have also come to the aid of quasi-Christian sects, including some branded as "evil

53. "Another Baby Slaughtered."

54. Wielander, *Christian Values*, 116–19.

55. Ma and Li, "Remaking the Civic Space," 17.

56. Lu, "Purdue Symposium."

cults" by the government, and have defended members of the banned Fa-lungong cult and advocates of greater freedom for Tibetans. In an overseas symposium on religious freedom in China, Chen Jiangang acknowledged that most such cases were politically rigged and the outcomes decided be-forehand; nonetheless, he argued that the value in taking these cases was in enhancing citizens' awareness of the lawful rights of these organizations. Another lawyer at the same symposium encouraged defense counsels who take up these cases to look for procedural loopholes in order to draw out the process, thus tying up more administrative resources and showing local officials that there is a cost associated with pursuing religious believers.[57]

For activist scholars, pastors, and defense lawyers, the line between rights advocacy and direct political action is a thin one, often unclear, fre-quently shifting, and ultimately defined by Party officials. Gao Zhisheng, named by the Ministry of Justice in 2001 as one of China's top ten lawyers, took on the cases of Falungong members and political activists, resulting in years of harassment for Gao and for his family members (who eventu-ally sought asylum in the United States). Gao was "disappeared" to China's far-west Xinjiang Province, deprived of all rights and subjected to horrific torture at the hands of the Chinese Communist Party.[58]

Most Christian scholars and pastors do not take their activism to this level. Instead, like generations of Chinese intellectuals before them, they build out their philosophical (and theological) frameworks in hopes that the regime will one day summon them from their think tanks and confer-ences and create a place for them to make a meaningful contribution to the task of national construction. Representing this stance, an article on the Chinese web site *Urban Mission* viewed the current Chinese govern-ment as being "transitional" (not yet modern, but no longer following the traditional Soviet model) and looked forward to the day when Chinese civil society will flourish, its middle class expand, and Christianity grow to nearly 250 million adherents. At this juncture, the article continued, the church is "prepared to deliver a covenant constitutional government."[59] This prescription calls to mind the recurring question that has long permeated discussions of Christian intellectual contributions to China's development, namely, whether Christianity is valuable because of its usefulness to China or whether it is to be valued in and of itself as a source of ultimate truth, in

57. Lu, "Purdue Symposium."
58. Conkling, "Mobilized Merchants—Patriotic Martyrs."
59. "Protestantism and the Future of China."

which case it is incumbent upon China to conform to the requirements of the Christian faith, not vice-versa.

Not all Christians in China are as committed to political change; in fact, most believers make it a point to stay clear of politics. Asked about the role of the church in society, a Christian journalist remarked that, at present, the church's strength was its relative smallness compared to China's larger population. To him, bigger is not necessarily better; the church needs to grow organically in order to become not simply larger but stronger. Most Christians, he claimed, are not comfortable talking about civil society, which he sees as a controversial topic within China's urban Christian community. While Christians should do good for the society, they should also remember that their real citizenship is in an eternal kingdom, and it is to this kingdom that they should bear witness. Democracy may emerge as a byproduct of Christian engagement, but it is not the job of the church to bring about democracy; other entities in society can do that.[60]

A scholar from a rural church background echoed these sentiments when he said that the church's caring for people in society will give the church legitimacy while at the same time setting apart the Christians from other socially active groups that are promoting democracy.[61] Another believer from a Christian intellectual family who grew up in an urban unregistered church warned, "While many aspects of the gospel can be helpful to the culture, if we don't preach salvation and sharply distinguish the gospel from 'good culture' our message will be eaten up by the culture." This believer emphasized the Christian cultural mandate is to live as salt and light within the prevailing culture, rather than either cooperating with or trying to overcome it. Historically, he said, Chinese Christian intellectuals have confused the cultural mandate with their own visions for the Chinese culture and nation.[62]

TRYING TO RUN BEFORE WALKING

Mary Ma and Li Jin's research on the increasingly public role of Christians in China led to their conclusion that, across multiple sectors, China's urban Christians are actively contributing toward the development of civil society: "What we have found is that the religious activities undertaken and values

60. Promise Hsu, interview with the author, October 9, 2014.

61. Yuan Hao, interview with the author, July 22, 2014.

62. W. E., interview with the author, July 13, 2014.

transmitted by Christian individuals, congregations, and faith-based associations have reshaped the local civil space in significant ways."[63] Another long-time observer of the church in China, however, is not so optimistic. He cautions that the church is still "finding itself" in terms of its role in society. "The church is trying to run before it can walk," perhaps trying to accomplish too much in the nonprofit sector without a sufficient level of internal maturity to be able to sustain the work.[64]

Ready or not, urbanization has thrust the church onto the stage of society, where it seeks to discover its identity while finding ways to express its faith practically through social engagement. Bringing with it a concentration of ideas and resources—intellectual and spiritual as well as material—and providing the technological support for the exchange of ideas and the building of relationships and networks, China's urbanization has created the conditions for the church to be, in scriptural terms, "salt and light" in a society that many would admit is in dire need of renewal.

63. Ma and Li, "Remarking the Civic Space," 15.
64. Y.M., interview with the author, July 8, 2014.

6

The Church's Global Mandate

"Go into all the world . . ."[1]

CHINA'S URBAN CHRISTIANS ARE more likely than their rural counterparts to have traveled overseas, studied or worked with individuals from outside China (perhaps even joining a foreign company or organization), or to have learned another language. As such they are thus more cognizant of the larger world beyond China's borders. With the Christian community in China becoming increasingly global in its outlook and better connected relationally (if not organizationally) to the global church, its leaders are seriously considering their role in the task of world evangelization. This cross-cultural vision is not new, either for the Chinese church globally or for China's church; however, the resources, connections and capabilities of the urban church are now making possible the emergence of a new missions movement from within China.

ANTECEDENTS FOR MISSIONS INVOLVEMENT

The current vision for cross-cultural missions within China is often traced back to the "Back to Jerusalem" movement of the 1940s. As documented by Paul Hattaway and others,[2] several church leaders in various parts of

1. Mark 16:15.
2. Yun et al., *Back to Jerusalem*.

China, independently of one another, reported sensing a specific call to take the gospel westward into China's predominately Muslim areas, into Central Asia, and beyond. Eventually a number of evangelistic bands were formed for this task. Probably the best known, albeit not the largest, was led by Zhao Maijia (Mecca Zhao) and his wife, He Enzheng. Known in missionary circles and outside China as "The Back to Jerusalem Band," it was called in Chinese, literally, "The Preach Everywhere Gospel Band." By 1949 workers had been dispatched to Gansu, Ningxia, Qinghai, Tibet, and Xinjiang. However, the work, which had already started to stagnate amidst China's civil war, came to a halt in 1949 after the Communist government seized control of Xinjiang. Following the Cultural Revolution the members of the band returned to Xinjiang, where many would remain and serve the church for decades.[3]

Meanwhile, as Western missionary efforts turned from China itself to the Chinese diaspora, and as the Chinese church matured in Hong Kong, Taiwan, Southeast Asia, North America, and elsewhere, there emerged a growing interest in cross-cultural missions among overseas Chinese Christians. This interest coincided with, and was strengthened by, the worldwide Lausanne movement, birthed at the eponymous congress in Switzerland in 1974, which was hosted by the Rev. Billy Graham and drew together evangelical leaders from around the world. Diaspora church leaders participated in early Lausanne congresses and, in 1976, held the first Chinese Congress on World Evangelization, now recognized as the watershed event in launching the contemporary overseas Chinese missions movement. In 1978 the Chinese Coordination Center of World Evangelization (CC-COWE) was created as the Chinese representation of the Lausanne movement. CCCOWE founder Dr. Thomas Wang, originally from Beijing, where he had been a disciple of Wang Mingdao, went on to chair the worldwide Lausanne II Congress in Manila in 1989.

In the past three decades much of the overseas Chinese church's missions efforts have, understandably, been directed toward Mainland China, where overseas Chinese Christians have been instrumental not only in providing pastoral training and other resources, but have also served as a "bridge" for numerous non-Chinese churches and organizations undertaking a variety of activities in China. It is this latter "bridge" function that is now proving significant to the growth of the indigenous missions movement in China, as overseas Chinese Christians serving in international

3. "The Preach Everywhere Gospel Band."

organizations become interpreters of culture for these organizations while at the same time conveying knowledge and skills from the international agencies to the church in China.

In the opinion of several overseas Chinese mission leaders interviewed for this book, the effectiveness of this diaspora missions effort has been mixed. On the one hand, as the outflow from greater China has resulted in Chinese going to nearly every country in the world, so the overseas Chinese church has been faithful to send workers to serve among these far-flung Chinese communities. In this sense it may be said that, at least geographically, overseas Chinese missionaries have managed to cross multiple barriers in an effort to spread the gospel. Along with existing denominational structures that included mission-sending functions, new specifically Chinese agencies and training institutions have been formed for this purpose. The resources of these entities and the collective experience of those sent out thus comprise a potential source of support for the cross-cultural missions movement emerging within China's urban church.

On the other hand, as most of the diaspora Chinese efforts have been directed toward other Chinese (one notable exception being work in the last couple decades among ethnic minorities in China), relatively few agencies and workers have actually undertaken the language and culture learning necessary for effective work in a completely foreign culture. Thus, while the overseas Chinese church may have much to offer in the way of training, organizational development, church relations, missions education, and care of workers and their families, the larger international Christian community may be more helpful to Christians in China in the area of cross-cultural preparation.[4]

A MANDATE FOR CHINA

An important factor in the genesis of the original "Preach Everywhere" band was the conviction that the Chinese church, having received the gospel from Western nations, owed a "gospel debt" to the rest of the world and thus had the responsibility to take the gospel to those places where it had yet to be received. This notion reemerged in the late 1990s as the "Back to Jerusalem" vision was rediscovered among churches (at that time primarily rural) in China. As this vision has been articulated in years since, it has often been stated as a unique mandate for the church in China: just as the

4. Kam, interview with the author, July 21, 2014.

Christian faith circumnavigated the globe from the Middle East to Europe, then to North America, and finally to Asia, now the baton has been passed to China to complete the journey back to Jerusalem. While Christians of various theological persuasions differ as to how literally to take this sense of divine mandate (and whether it in fact has any biblical basis), the idea that it is "our turn" animates the thinking of many in the contemporary church in China who promote the church's role in cross-cultural missions, perhaps in a manner similar to the sense of destiny that characterized South Korea's significant missions sending thrust in the 1980s.

Another impetus for missions was voiced by a pastor in a major city in China, who advised that an outward focus on extending the influence of the gospel to the ends of the earth was critical to the church's future development. Without this, he said, Christianity in China would begin to die out, as it has in some Western nations: "We only know how to consider development from the point of view of the church's own interests and needs, yet have failed to take into account that the mission of the church is evangelism: to take the gospel of Jesus Christ to the ends of the earth. To meet the church's own needs, or to share the gospel: these are two completely different driving forces for development."[5]

SMALL BEGINNINGS

The reality of current cross-cultural efforts emanating from within China's church speaks of small beginnings inspired by big vision. One urban leader reasons that, since China in the past received a total of about 20,000 missionaries from abroad, Christians in China should be able to send out that many as well. Setting the year 2030 as the target for this goal to be reached, he recommends starting locally by working among ethnic groups within China's borders while simultaneously preparing to send workers abroad. Although pastors from various parts of China have been meeting to discuss cross-cultural work for at least the past decade, one observer says there are currently only about a half dozen leaders who have emerged as champions of the cause. Contrary to some reports, well publicized in the West, that boast of upward of 100,000 missionaries being sent out of China, the current numbers are more likely in the hundreds. According to one mission leader within China, most of those who have been sent abroad have gone to

5. "Evangelism and Missions."

Africa or South Asia. Very few of these have remained for longer than two years, for reasons that will be examined later in this chapter.[6]

Nonetheless, the small steps taken to date have been significant. These include launching indigenous agencies to recruit and send workers, establishing missionary training institutions, introducing missions-related courses in existing unofficial seminaries and Bible schools, collaboration among church congregations to train and send their members, conferences and missions education programs for churches, and starting businesses in ethnic minority areas or in other countries in order to support Christian outreach. Christian leaders from across China meet regularly on their own initiative to discuss ways of mobilizing missionaries from within China. A *Christian Times* article told of a church service in Anhui province where Chinese missionaries who had served in Laos, Pakistan, and Cambodia came together to share their experiences with the congregation. The couple serving in Laos were in their fifties and had, with no prior culinary training, opened a small restaurant as a means of maintaining a presence in the region. A young couple returning from Pakistan told of building homes for those who had been affected by a major flood. They challenged the congregation in Anhui, "The Chinese church does not lack people or money. What we lack is love."[7]

AN URBAN LAUNCHPAD

Although it was possible in the 1980s and 1990s for rural church leaders to "parachute" into cities or even locations abroad for brief meetings with their counterparts in other churches or networks, or with Christians outside China, for the most part these rural leaders were landlocked both geographically and culturally. China's cities (not to mention places outside China) were another world, and the entire frame of reference of these Christians was shaped by their experience as rural peasants (and in some cases further defined by their identification with a particular region having its own dialect and culturally distinct features). The urban transformation of these networks has made interaction with one another, and with Christians from outside China, commonplace, allowing for joint planning, mutual learning, and sharing of resources. With more relationships come more possibilities. Chinese Christians seeking to serve cross culturally are not

6. Kam, interview with the author, July 21, 2014.
7. "Overseas Missions."

limited just to opportunities offered within their immediate church circles but can weigh a variety of options before deciding where to get involved.

Meanwhile the emerging urban Christian community contains many highly educated believers who speak English and other languages, not a few of whom have studied or worked abroad. Their relational networks extend to other cities within China and to nations beyond, creating natural bridges for cooperation with international organizations involved in cross-cultural missions. More foreign China-based workers from these international organizations are found in the cities as opposed to the countryside. With the urbanization of the church have come greater opportunities for these workers to assist local Christian leaders in the area of cross-cultural equipping and sending. China's cities have taken on more of the cosmopolitan nature characteristic of similar cities in other parts of the world as China has urbanized, bringing China's Christians face to face with people of other ethnic backgrounds, be they migrants from China's minority areas or business people, professionals or students from other countries.

The increased mobility and diversity brought about through urbanization have also fostered internal changes that have served to better position the church for cross-cultural involvement. Formerly a resource-starved, largely marginalized peasant movement, the church now possesses considerable financial means thanks to the relatively well-off status of its urban members. The pastor mentioned earlier who formulated the "2030" vision listed China's economic growth as a key resource for the church's development of cross-cultural missions. As for human assets, the church has gone from having a fairly limited repertoire of ministry tools and approaches to possessing a variety of skills within its ranks. Those trained in media, for example, can use their talents to raise awareness and mobilize Christians for cross-cultural service. Publishers can likewise help educate and produce training materials. Entrepreneurs can create business platforms for those going abroad or into remote regions of China. Christians with organizational skills are able to contribute to the development of new entities created to recruit, train, and send workers. Believers trained in counseling can be involved in the screening and emotional preparation and care of workers. The shift away from a hierarchical, top-down church structure discussed in previous chapters means that these assets are available to be used by diverse Christian groups whose various efforts complement one another.

Finally, the increased mobility and connectedness of China's urban Christian community along with these internal transformations have changed the way in which it relates to the larger Christian body outside China. Chinese Christians have moved from being largely dependent upon outside resources to being, in many respects, self-sustaining. International organizations have played and are playing a significant role in informal ways such as offering counsel, interacting with Chinese Christians in international conferences, and allowing existing missions-related training materials to be translated into Chinese. Foreign workers serving with these agencies in China may be mentors to Chinese Christians interested in cross-cultural work. More formal partnership comes through training conducted by the agencies, either inside China or elsewhere in Asia, through placement of Chinese workers in international teams working among ethnic groups in China or abroad, through coaching in areas such as mobilization or agency management, or through sponsorship of indigenous mission agencies. Outside involvement is less about financial support and more about sharing expertise.

One international organization, for example, is able to aid in the development of a local agency in China focused on sending workers to a particular ethnic group by providing mentoring and some limited financial support. As part of their training, personnel from the local agency are invited to serve for a period alongside their counterparts in the international organization. Together, the leadership from both entities decides what policies and procedures developed by the international organization might (or might not) be appropriate for use in China. Although the outside organization may see this agency somewhat as an extension of its own international work, the local agency maintains its autonomy. Rather than replicating itself in China, the international agency is collaborating with Christian leaders in China to create something new that is a unique extension of the Chinese church.

PERCEIVED CHALLENGES

In many ways, the urbanization of the church has made possible these advances in the area of cross-cultural missions. Yet Christian leaders in China would be quick to acknowledge the challenges that remain, both within the community and in how it relates externally. One challenge is simply a lack of understanding within the church of its responsibility in the area of cross-cultural mission. Despite the rhetoric among some pastors about engaging in cross-cultural work, most congregations are more than fully occupied with their own immediate local concerns. Leaders, particularly those who have been Christians for a relatively short period of time, may not be equipped to articulate to their congregations the biblical basis for the church's cross-cultural mandate. One pastor, writing in the online Christian magazine *Church China*, remarked, "Some Chinese preachers are too narrow-minded and have no interest in mission, while others want to do it but don't know where to start. This reveals that the Chinese church is still very fragmented, lacking cohesion over the issue of missions."[8] This pastor and others like him would thus see missions education as a primary task to be undertaken at the local church level, supplemented by activities such as citywide or regional conferences for missions awareness and mobilization.

Secondly, current cross-cultural efforts undertaken by China's urban Christians tend to be piecemeal. These may consist variously of sending short-term teams to ethnic groups within China or beyond China's borders, providing missions education within the church, supporting workers sent out, or establishing Christian-run businesses in a target area. All of these activities are necessary in the overall cross-cultural effort, but none is sufficient in and of itself. Lacking a comprehensive view of how these various pieces fit together to comprise the whole, individual congregations may spend considerable energy on one aspect of cross-cultural missions, only to find that their attempts flounder because they lack the complementary components required for success.

Training, for example, without the means to send workers out, results in members gaining knowledge and being infused with zeal, but with nowhere to go in order to put into practice what they have learned. Sending out workers without a proper support structure to sustain them once they reach their destination reduces the likelihood that they will be able to stay for any length of time. While it is true that different church congregations and other entities may have different roles to play, these component efforts need a degree of coordination if they are all to contribute toward a sustainable comprehensive effort. To this end urban Christian leaders from various cities have been intentionally meeting together to discuss how existing initiatives might be better coordinated and to identify gaps that have yet to be addressed.

Very few leaders within the urban church community have proven cross-cultural skills. Given that the majority of Christians are Han Chinese

8. "Evangelism and Missions."

(or members of China's ethnic Korean minority), steeped in the predominant Han culture, with little opportunity or need to interact with others different than themselves, it is not surprising that they should lack cross-cultural experience. Up until recently some pastors in China would disregard work among China's ethnic minorities, ostensibly for the reason that they would not contribute to the growth of the Chinese church. The Chinese pastor quoted in *Church China,* above, called on his fellow Chinese Christians to "renew our thinking, destroying our Jonah-like nationalism, narrow individualism, and 'Sino-centrism.'"[9]

In her critique of contemporary missionary efforts, Gerda Wielander contrasts the work of Republican era Western missionaries, who elevated the status of minority peoples such as the Miao and Lisu by translating the Bible into their own languages, with that of contemporary Chinese missionaries, who use the Chinese Bible and preach in *Putonghua* (Mandarin). In Wielander's view, these missionary endeavors, rather than strengthening the minorities' ethnic identity, reinforce the Chinese government's own campaign to "liberate" minorities from cultural and economic backwardness.[10]

Missionary immersion in other cultures, whether inside or outside China, has been difficult since, even in these situations, it is easier to relate to other Chinese than to integrate into a new host culture. Chinese Christians' natural use of the Chinese language, traditional relational styles, culture, and habits (such as eating pork) can unwittingly become serious barriers to meaningful cross-cultural interaction unless deliberate attempts are made to put aside these default behaviors and become learners in a new environment.

INTERNATIONAL COLLABORATION: POSSIBILITIES AND OBSTACLES

Collaborating with international agencies may be helpful in overcoming this lack of cross-cultural experience. Currently a handful of urban church members are serving in internships with such agencies, where they encounter not only the challenge of working in new cross-cultural settings but also the added challenge of doing so as part of a team that is itself made up of people from a different culture or perhaps multiple cultures.

9. Ibid.
10. Wielander, "Researching Chinese Christianity."

Various models of relating to the international entity have been proposed, from joining the agency directly as individual members to forming an indigenous agency under the tutelage of the foreign counterpart and then, as the indigenous agency matures, collaborating as peers. Other individual congregations, networks, or fellowships of churches in China may choose to send their own members independently but then collaborate with workers from international agencies who are already serving in the host culture. Whatever the model, early attempts at collaboration have shown the difficulties in connecting with the international missions movement.

Given the relatively opaque nature of China's unregistered church, international organizations have found it difficult to know where to connect. Chinese representation at several high-profile international conferences in recent years has ostensibly helped to bring together those from within China who have a cross-cultural vision with those from abroad who are seeking to partner with them. At the same time, however, these attempts have exposed areas of division within the church in China. In the late 2000s a group of pastors from several cities along with recognized leaders of some of the larger rural unregistered church networks began making plans for some 200 Christian leaders from China to attend Cape Town 2010, an international Christian conference held in South Africa under the auspices of the Lausanne Movement. Endeavoring to gather a contingent that would represent the diversity of the unregistered church, the organizers in China sought to draw from four major categories: 1) traditional urban churches, 2) traditional rural networks, 3) newly emerged urban congregations (both among young professionals and migrant workers), and 4) Christian professionals in business, media, the arts and others sectors.[11] Significant funds were raised from churches and individual believers within China to enable these leaders to attend, as well as to provide scholarships for participants from other developing nations.

Although virtually all of those invited were, in the end, not allowed to leave China to attend the conference, organizers believed the process leading up to the gathering, which involved years of meeting quietly with Christian leaders from diverse backgrounds and theological persuasions, was as valuable, if not more valuable, than the benefit of participating in the conference itself. This process furthered significantly the development of a nationwide network comprising rural and urban, traditional and newly emerged, charismatic and Reformed Christians. (Other Christian leaders

---

11. Enoch Kim, interview with the author, November 22, 2014.

in China, however, did not agree with the selection process or with making participation in an international conference such a high-profile goal, and criticized the proceedings as being ultimately divisive.) Among those leaders who have participated in this network, and the groups they represent, continued interaction within China as well as through international forums has fostered not only communication and the exchange of resources but also practical collaboration in the area of Chinese cross-cultural missions involvement. Around 100 leaders who were not able to attend Cape Town 2010 did participate in a subsequent Lausanne-sponsored event in Seoul in 2013, where they joined to issue a statement affirming their commitment to "maintaining the unity of the Spirit in the bond of peace" and to "joining hands with the global church in world missions."[12]

Although in 2010 the connection to a larger international movement helped foster unity within the Chinese church, the conspicuous absence of TSPM participation in what was billed as "the most representative gathering of the Christian church in history," as well as the inability of the unregistered church invitees to attend, highlight the ongoing obstacles to inter-church and international cooperation posed by China's current religious policy. The Lausanne international leadership's official invitation to the TSPM leadership was refused, ostensibly because they were not willing to sign the Lausanne Covenant, a document affirming commitment to world evangelization with which all conference participants were expected to concur. As China's religious policy does not permit evangelism outside officially designated sites, the TSPM cannot agree with the Lausanne position on spreading the gospel. Lausanne leaders responded by offering "observer" status to TSPM representatives. However, the prospect of unregistered church leaders attending as full participants while they took a back seat at the conference was obviously not palatable to TSPM leaders, who saw Lausanne's compromise proposal as not only a loss of face but also a direct challenge to government policy. The opening night in Cape Town thus resembled the scene twenty years earlier at a previous Lausanne conference in Manila, where, in the wake of the Tiananmen tragedy, 200 empty seats signified the absence of delegates from China.[13]

International gatherings such as these invariably raise the question of who speaks for the church in China. The participants who are able to get to the venue, who are able to be heard by virtue of being more outspoken

12. "Seoul Commitment."
13. Cresswell, "What Future?"

or having better English language ability, or who know the organizers of the meeting may not be those who are best prepared to interact with the international community in cross-cultural work. Some who may appear to the foreign community to be leaders may not have the support of the masses of Christians inside China. Participants from urban and rural backgrounds may approach cross-cultural work from very different perspectives (urban leaders, for example, taking a more methodological approach and giving close attention to matters such as obtaining visas, while rural leaders just want to get to the field).[14] Building relationships takes time. Becoming acquainted in international gatherings may provide an entry point, but international organizations that are serious about pursuing long-term collaboration with cross-cultural workers in China will need to invest in building understanding and clarifying expectations, taking seriously the reality that working with the church in China is in itself a cross-cultural endeavor.

Even where international agencies have been able to form strong relationships with individuals committed to cross-cultural work, it is difficult for these agencies, unless they have a long history of China involvement, to understand the complex church backgrounds of those with whom they are working. While these individuals may themselves have a clear sense of purpose, the Christian communities to which they belong are juggling a host of internal challenges and domestic ministry commitments. Thus Christians from China may not be as committed to, or prepared for, cross-cultural work as the international agency expects them to be. Coming from a "managerial missions" perspective, the international agency may emphasize tangible results while downplaying attributes, such as a deep dependence on God and a willingness to suffer, which are at the core of the Chinese church's identity.

On the other side, Chinese church leaders may expect the international agency to underwrite the cost of training, sending and supporting workers sent out from China, while agencies assume that the church in China will bear this responsibility. The financial relationship between churches in China and international organizations is fraught with pitfalls. In the words of one longtime observer, the fact that much of this early work has been funded by overseas organizations threatens to curtail the development of a truly indigenous missiology by perpetuating the false assumption that missions is the purview of the church outside China. Another leader involved in training workers in China remarked that some international agencies

14. Kam, interview with the author, July 21, 2014.

have been accused of "cherry picking" the most talented leaders in China by offering them high salaries to join their teams.[15]

Despite the rapidly rising standard of living in urban China, economic disparity between the international organization and Chinese church can be a major sticking point in attempts to collaborate. The experience of international agencies tells them that sending and maintaining workers on the field is a complex and costly endeavor. Church leaders from China look at budget items such as medical insurance, tuition for children's education, and retirement funds and conclude that this foreign model does not fit their own situation. This disconnect may be accentuated by a martyr mentality among some Chinese Christians, who believe their role is simply to "go and die."[16] Even if items such as ensuring that their children receive a proper education are acknowledged as valid, the ways in which they approach these requirements may be very different from those of their international partners. In the areas of finance and organizational structure, international partnerships can provide guidance and helpful models, but China's urban Christian leaders must ultimately decide what actually fits their situation the best.

Leadership arrangements comprise another difficult area in collaboration between Chinese and foreign entities. Once workers get to the field, are they accountable to congregations back in China, to team members from international organizations with whom they serve, or to the international agency itself? The potential for conflicting loyalties is obvious. In one case, a worker from China working under international leadership received permission to purchase a used vehicle and the funds with which to do so. When his sending church in China also sent money he decided to buy a new vehicle instead, whereupon the international agency reprimanded him for not following instructions. The worker, in turn, took the car and struck out on his own.[17] Such are the complications that can arise when Chinese *guanxi* relationships collide with foreign organizational procedures. The potential for similar conflicts exists in decisions about which requirements are necessary for workers to be accepted for cross-cultural service, where they are to be sent, the composition of teams, and who should play which roles on the team, among other areas.

In spite of the conflicts inherent in collaboration with international agencies, their years of experience are seen as valuable by Chinese

15. L. W., interview with the author, July 9, 2014.
16. Ibid.
17. W. T., interview with the author, July 23, 2014.

Christians who are pioneers in cross-cultural work. In the words of one of these pioneers, even bad experiences, if we can learn from them, are better than no experience at all.

The biggest obstacle, according to one urban Christian who has studied internationally and now leads a cross-cultural sending organization within China, is the inability of churches to cooperate, and of workers to get along with one another and with foreign partnering organizations. On the China side, denominational differences prevent some congregations or groups of congregations from working with others. This leader complained that pastors often ask about the denominational identity of his organization. Some, when they hear that his organization is interdenominational, refuse to work with him, and, of these, some have subsequently started similar agencies to serve only those within their denomination. When they reach the field, however, workers from various church backgrounds are forced to serve together. Without the blessing of their churches back home to do so, and with no prior experience in collaborating with people from other churches, their inability to cooperate becomes a major obstacle. In the experience of this particular leader, many of those sent out to work in teams eventually leave the team, and most of these eventually return home.[18] This difficulty points up a key issue identified by many urban Christian leaders, which will be explored further in the following chapter.

RURAL LEGACY, URBAN RESOURCES

The Chinese church's vision for cross-cultural missions is not new, but the emergence of a new type of urban church may prove significant in making this desire a reality. Possessing a unique collection of connections, resources, experiences, and abilities, China's urban Christians bring to the cross-cultural task both a new way of thinking about and relating to the world, and the practical means of working cross-culturally. Still one may argue that the rural church, which has long been the torchbearer of China's evangelistic vision, possesses a missionary zeal that has yet to permeate the fabric of China's relatively young urban congregations. Lacking this intrinsic motivation and drawing (perhaps unconsciously) instead on a Confucian desire to succeed, the urban church may take on cross-cultural missions as yet another addition to its growing repertoire of programs, employing managerial techniques and well-funded initiatives but failing

18. W. T., interview with the author, July 23, 2014.

to truly engage the hearts and minds of church members in the missions endeavor.[19] Merely copying the operational procedures of international partners without fully grasping the rationale behind these practices could accentuate this tendency.

Hence the need for effective partnership between urban leaders, who are fast becoming the vanguard of China's church, and those rural leaders of a previous generation whose missionary zeal was born out of their experience of suffering and a life of simple devotion. This will require humility on the part of urban Christians, who, according to Gerda Wielander, demonstrate skepticism toward the faith healings, dreams and visions, and other "superstitious" traditions of their rural counterparts, viewing some rural groups as "backward, unenlightened and dangerous."[20] At the same time, rural leaders will need themselves to demonstrate humility toward the newer urban leadership, recognizing the unique resources that the urban church brings to the missionary task.

19. Enoch Kim, interview with the author, November 22, 2014.
20. Wielander, "Researching Chinese Christianity."

7

The Quest for Unity

"that they may be one . . ."[1]

URBANIZATION HAS CREATED THE conditions for China's Christians to work together in new ways. Transportation links, greater social mobility, and relaxed controls on the church allow believers to connect physically. The growth of China's commercial sector further opens up social space for Christian interaction. Old and new institutions, whether universities or nascent think tanks or media entities, serve as hubs for the concentration of intellectual resources and the dissemination of ideas. New technologies facilitate this dissemination. With globalization comes participation in international networks, bringing together believers from various cities, backgrounds and church affiliations. Urban migration, meanwhile, forces those from the countryside to find new social support systems, breaking down traditional church loyalties and creating new migrant Christian communities. All of these factors open up new avenues for collaboration and new possibilities in the minds of younger Christian leaders, most of them first-generation believers, who have managed to shed much of the cultural and historical baggage that, in the past, served to perpetuate division among Chinese Christians.

Whereas rural church networks had, to some degree, functioned as *de facto* denominations, providing an overarching structure whereby individual churches could relate to one another, urban congregations have

1. John 17:22.

traditionally remained rather isolated. Individual TSPM churches related to one another formally within the context of their city or provincial TSPM/CCC structures, but actual collaboration between churches was not necessarily encouraged, nor was interaction with unregistered congregations in the city. For security reasons, the unregistered congregations kept a low profile. A lack of trust between individual church leaders and the knowledge that local security officials were keeping a watchful eye on their activities prevented these pastors from pursuing open collaboration. As rural networks and Wenzhou church plants began moving into the cities they brought with them new sets of relationships that allowed for greater interaction among leaders within their respective circles.

Meanwhile, a new generation of urban Christian leaders began to emerge at the beginning of this century, establishing collegial relationships that allowed for the formation of city-wide pastors' prayer fellowships. Several of these leaders also participated in training opportunities, in some cases facilitated by Christians from outside China, which provided the neutral ground on which they could build friendships. These personal relationships laid the foundation for the collaboration that would emerge following the Wenchuan earthquake in May 2008, when congregations from at least 15 cities joined forces to send volunteers and relief supplies to the disaster zone. Further collaboration has been ongoing in areas such as theological training and the equipping and sending of Chinese missionaries to ethnic minorities within China and beyond China's borders.

As the theological sophistication of this generation of leaders has increased, and as they have struggled to address the structural issues facing the church, they have gone beyond simple networking and collaborating on projects to form "federation"-type structures and, in some cases, embryonic presbyteries linking together congregations in multiple cities within a given geographical region. One such grouping emerged naturally out of a group of relatively young urban congregations that had been planted with the help of trainers from a particular denomination outside China. Although these trainers did not expect that the congregations in China would take on the identity of their denomination, nor did they encourage them to do so, nonetheless these young pastors chose to adopt both the denominational identity as well as its form of church government. They are currently in the process of forming what will likely be a presbytery comprising their individual congregations. Groups of pastors in other parts of China are following suit. While the move toward more formal relationships between these emerging urban church congregations is still very much in its infancy, it is a trend that could significantly affect how they identify with one another and with society.

THE NEED FOR UNITY

As new ways of relating to one another have become possible, China's urban Christians have identified unity as a key concern. The motivations for this unity are complex and interrelated, rooted not only in pragmatic concerns but also in the biblical teaching that they should "all be one" in Jesus Christ, and that the quality of their Christian witness is a direct function of this unity.[2] The Pauline epistles refer to this unity in various contexts, particularly in Paul's letter to the Philippian church, where he repeatedly uses the Greek term *koinonia* in various forms, taking the relationship of Jesus Christ, God the Father, and the Holy Spirit within the Trinity as indicative of the intimate sharing that should characterize not only the individual believer's relationship to Christ but also relationships among Christians themselves.[3] The obstacles to Christian unity are also complex and interrelated, involving cultural elements, the church's relationship to the government and to entities outside China, generational differences, and much history that continues to influence relations within the church today. To address these obstacles urban church leaders are exploring a variety of new structural approaches, including the formation of denominations, which can bring about needed cohesiveness but which also pose new obstacles to unity.

Speaking to a group of Chinese and international Christian leaders, Li Shengfeng, pastor of Beijing City Revival Church, implored that "the most important thing for the Chinese church is unity." For Li, it is this unity that will bring about mission, enabling the Chinese church to fulfill its God-given purpose of engaging in cross-cultural outreach. Using the analogy of a football team, Li said, "We're all on the same team. We need to work together so we can play a good game."[4] David Ro, Missions Director at the Gordon Conwell Theological Seminary's J. Christy Wilson Center

2. John 17:20–21.

3. Philippians 1:5; 3:10; 4:14–15.

4. Conversation with the author, July 27, 2013.

for Missions Studies, notes that, as Christians realize they need to come together in order to expand beyond their own local context, they then see the need to collaborate with Christians inside and outside China. This unity, however, entails risk, as more Christians coming together in a more visible manner will result in greater scrutiny of the church. On the other hand, wanting to be recognized in the public sphere, which many urban church leaders believe is vital to the church's witness to society, requires having visible unity.[5]

In many spheres of Christian endeavor, there is an awareness that individual congregations may be doing good work but lack coordination among themselves. City churches attempting work among China's ethnic minority peoples, for example, may not be aware of who else is working among the same people group or in the same region. This unity is also necessary for the church—particularly the unregistered church—to stand against opposition. China's urban unregistered church leaders do not see the government as the enemy. However, they do believe that, as they become more united, they will encounter spiritual warfare and thus experience opposition, including at the hands of the government. Several urban church leaders mentioned the Shouwang "storm" as an example of churches standing together. Although Shouwang Church was on the frontlines, facing direct opposition for its confrontational stand vis-à-vis the Beijing city government, other pastors in the city and beyond stood with the congregation in prayer and by offering moral and practical support. This conflict was seen not just as Shouwang's battle, but as a struggle involving the unregistered church as a whole.[6]

OBSTACLES TO UNITY

Particularly among unregistered churches, individual congregations in the city have tended to function as "little islands," each self-sufficient and focused primarily on its own needs. The physical and structural isolation of urban congregations and their leaders has both external and internal causes. China's religious policy has effectively forced unregistered groups to stay small and disconnected, as any attempts to grow too large or to form networks could be seen as a threat, thus drawing unwanted attention from authorities. The resulting culture of secrecy mitigates against open

5. David Ro, interview with the author, August 12, 2014.
6. Lu, "Purdue Symposium."

collaboration between churches. Given the rapid growth of the church and the corresponding lack of trained leaders, most congregations have been perpetually shorthanded and too busy dealing with internal issues to spend much time building relationships outside the church. Within larger churches or networks of churches (some of the traditional rural networks that have established congregations among urban migrants, for example) people tend to become "siloed," focusing on their particular ministry tasks to the point that collaboration even within the congregation is difficult.

Geographical, class, and generational differences exacerbate the isolation. Traditional urban churches with older members, for example, would find it challenging to relate to some of the newly emerging congregations where most members tend to be young, well-educated professionals, not a few of whom have studied or worked overseas. Such churches may be viewed as too willing to take risks or too quick to adopt new approaches to ministry. Congregations of urban migrant workers, many of which have ties to rural networks, would tend not to relate to churches among China's growing urban middle class or among working class believers who have a long history in the city. Even among registered church congregations, joined together by the TSPM structure, believers of different social classes tend to worship in different churches depending on geography and their respective work schedules.

No one body or organization in China has the authority to convene believers from different churches. It would be awkward for any one leader to take this role upon his- or herself, as doing so could be perceived as a symptom of pride or an attempt to recruit others to a particular agenda. Where this kind of convening has taken place, it has largely been around some shared resource, such as a training course, often brought in by an outside or foreign entity. In cities where the TSPM and the unregistered churches have an agreeable relationship the TSPM may play this role by organizing classes that are open to members of unregistered groups or by supplying Bibles or other resources to the church at large. A few large unregistered seminaries have sizeable alumni networks that also can facilitate cooperation across churches. In this culture of relative isolation there have historically been few models of leaders working together. Absent such models, efforts at collaboration have been difficult even where there has been a desire on the part of leaders to seek and to demonstrate unity.

Cultural factors play a significant role in the struggle for unity. In talking with Chinese Christians about the perceived need for unity, this author heard more than one interviewee resort to a rather unflattering Chinese idiom: "One Chinese, a dragon; three Chinese, a worm" (*yige zhongguoren, yi tiao long; sange zhongguoren, yi tiao chong*). In other words, a single Chinese may be perceived as being very capable, but this effectiveness disappears when teamwork is required. Chinese social relationships are characterized by a lack of trust. When dealing with a stranger, the default posture is to assume the worst about the other person. The legacy of the Cultural Revolution, with government-sanctioned class struggle pitting children against parents and tearing apart friendships and marriages, was that people built walls around themselves for self-protection.[7] In the decades since, China has made huge strides economically, significantly raising the standard of living for hundreds of millions of people, yet trust remains a rare commodity. Relationships among Christians are no exception, with the lack of trust further exacerbated by the aura of secrecy and lack of accountability structures that has characterized the unregistered church in particular.

Without the ability to legally register and to open a bank account in the name of the church, for example, the congregation must resort to entrusting a leader or other responsible individual to manage the church's money. Comingling of church funds with personal funds becomes a common practice, leading to accusations of misuse. In the case of Wenzhou's "boss Christians," the line between church and business funds may shift depending upon the needs of the church or the business. Although more robust accountability systems are beginning to be seen in the newer urban congregations, the handling of finances remains a sensitive area.

Another common cultural barrier to unity mentioned among Christians is a desire to control and a corresponding fear of being controlled. Leaders often speak of "mountaintop-ism" (*shanding zhuyi*), referring to the tendency of pastors to each be the master of his own territory, which he carefully protects. The idea of allowing others to give input into one's own ministry is thus perceived as threatening.[8] Success in ministry, seen in terms of greater influence and a larger congregation, is a zero-sum game. There is scant incentive to work together, unless by doing so a leader perceives that his church will benefit.

The tendency of leaders not to want to work together is related to a tradition of conflict avoidance. Since conflict inevitably results in a loss of face, it is better not to attempt to work together if it could cause conflict.

7. M. D., interview with the author, July 4, 2014.

8. Fulton, "Healthy Partnering."

In the absence of structures for dealing with conflict, such as feedback mechanisms or procedures for voting within a group, people hide their true feelings and ideas in order to preserve face. It is difficult to discuss ideas objectively or to provide constructive criticism, since the idea and the person suggesting it are inextricably linked; by criticizing the idea one is also criticizing the person. When a problem finally does surface, much time and effort are then required to solve it. The need for face thus reinforces the isolation of leaders and the notion that it is safer to work alone in one's own territory then to attempt to work in a shared space with others.[9]

THEOLOGICAL FAULT LINES

Doctrinal differences constitute a third major obstacle to unity. Here the two main dividing lines within the Chinese church are between the Calvinist (emphasizing God's unconditional election of those who receive salvation) and Arminian (emphasizing human free will) positions, and between charismatic, or Pentecostal, and non-charismatic believers. Some ultra-Reformed groups in China's cities have been criticized for becoming extremely exclusive and causing disunity.[10] A number of years ago the tension between the Calvinist and Arminian positions came to a head in Wenzhou, resulting in a major split. As Lian Xi has pointed out, several major indigenous Christian movements that emerged in China in the early 20th century were markedly Pentecostal in nature, characterized by divine healing, exorcism, and ecstatic worship. These influenced the later development of China's rural house church networks.[11]

Examining similarities between these charismatic practices and traditional Chinese folk practices, Timothy Conkling concluded, "One of the primary factors that explains the growth of the house-church movement in the PRC is the affinity that exists between the practices and goals represented in Chinese traditional folk-religions, especially as they are practiced in China's rural areas, and the practices of seeking healing and exorcism through methods commonly practiced in charismatic Protestant Christianity."[12] Conkling's research in Henan province revealed that more than 90 percent of believers traced their conversions directly to a miraculous healing, and

9. Mary Ma, interview with the author, August 15, 2014.
10. David Ro, interview with the author, August 12, 2014.
11. Xi, *Redeemed by Fire*, 215–20.
12. Conkling, *Mobilized Merchants—Patriotic Martyrs*.

they also saw a relationship between healing and church growth. According to Conkling, "The animistic, superstitious world-view of a typical rural farmer coincided with charismatic Christianity in its shared emphasis on the goal of religious practice to bring blessing, help, and healing in this present life." Conkling contrasted this charismatic faith with the liturgical, clergy-driven Christianity that had developed in China during the first half of the 20th century but never was able to establish deep roots.[13]

This more formal Christianity bears similarity to the growing Reformed tradition currently gaining a foothold in China's cities, particularly among the well-educated, who often look with skepticism upon the "superstitious" practices of their rural brothers and sisters. The Reformed emphasis on rational thinking and systematic theology tends to discount the "emotional" and "mystical" spirituality of China's traditional, particularly rural, churches. One Chinese pastor observed in an online Christian publication:

> [A]n important problem is that many of these Reformed urban churches do not have an overlapping older spiritual generation from which to inherit. On top of that, there are many intellectuals in these churches, so they are susceptible to the trap of rationality and reason. Reformed thought itself is very rational and logical. So it's not surprising that, because of its developed thought and the lack of overlap with living spiritual predecessors, combined with an innate deficiency, people feel as if the people of the Reformed church are very rational, enjoy debating and critiquing people, and that all conversation is logical, coherent, and about the law."[14]

DOCTRINAL DIFFERENCES AND EDUCATIONAL CULTURE

Current divisions over doctrine may be seen as being rooted in the particular nature of theological education in China and, at a deeper level, in cultural attitudes toward education in general. Since Chinese education has traditionally emphasized rote learning, the stress has been on knowing the "correct" answers rather than on analytical or creative tasks. In theological education, there has likewise been a tendency to teach a particular "correct" approach to doctrine as the only legitimate one. Jackson Wu, writing about

13. Ibid.
14. "Interview with a Reformed Church Pastor (2)."

Chinese ecclesiology, makes the observation, "It is not uncommon to hear Christian leaders misunderstand church history and ways of speaking such that authority is vested almost blindly in one school of thought or another." Wu goes on to recount a conversation with a registered church pastor who expressed shock at the idea that being a "Calvinist" did not mean one followed everything Calvin said.[15]

Foreign teachers from various denominational backgrounds, many of them overseas Chinese from Hong Kong, Taiwan or North America, or Christian workers from South Korea, have had considerable influence in the past three decades as they have endeavored to assist in training a new generation of church leaders. Coming from different theological traditions, they have, often unwittingly, contributed toward the sharpening of doctrinal differences between various groups of believers. Rather than learning where the theological "river banks" lie, within which may be found various shades of interpretation that could all be considered orthodox, their students in China instead come to view doctrine as an exact science. The result is exclusivity, highlighting fine lines of division rather than broad areas of common belief and thus creating barriers to cooperation.

Lacking knowledge of the historical background of a particular position to which they subscribe, as well as an understanding of where this position fits within the larger theological spectrum, some leaders in China may end up adhering to a position that is even more extreme than that held by their mentors and teachers outside China. These outside sponsors may, in turn, "brand" their trainees as their church's or denomination's representatives in China, not realizing that the version that is being practiced in China may have become in some ways a caricature of the original.[16] One American Christian living in China tells of a conversation in a bookstore with a young local believer who proudly announced that he was part of a PCA (Presbyterian Church in America) fellowship in town, and that Reformed theology was "the one ancient and faithful reception of the biblical faith."[17] (It goes without saying that, in the eyes of government leaders, such foreign denominational connections bring back to China all the unwanted baggage associated with the missionary era.)

On the other extreme are many expatriate Christians serving in China who have emphasized evangelism and personal spiritual development but

15. Wu, "Authority," 13.
16. Y. M., interview with the author, July 8, 2014.
17. Swells, "Calvinism."

have not given much attention to matters of church polity or correct doctrine, often because these were not emphasized in their own development as Christians or were not a priority for the organizations or churches that sent them to China. When their converts eventually move into church leadership they find themselves at a loss to adequately articulate their own theological position and to prescribe suitable practices for the church, creating ambiguity internally and making it difficult to work with peers whose own positions are more clearly defined.

Given the difficulties that doctrinal differences can pose, the quest for unity may itself be an obstacle to unity. According to one Christian intellectual with an urban unregistered church background, harmony (a traditional Chinese virtue) and love are priorities of the church and are perhaps over-preached. Stressing unity above all else does not allow for open discussion of theology and theological differences. Yet, if these are not brought out into the open, the basis for unity cannot be clearly established and the underlying but unspoken differences will invariably cause friction.[18] Hence the importance for congregations and their leaders to define the bottom line, namely, those areas of doctrine, practice, and ministry priorities on which they are able to unify.[19]

THE POLITICAL DIVIDE

The most obvious area of division within the church remains the divide between believers in China's official church, operating under the auspices of the Three Self Patriotic Movement, and those in the unregistered church. Within the unregistered church a related area of division exists around the question of if, and how, the church should relate to the government. With China's reform and opening have come significant changes in the TSPM's role, in China's religious policy, and in the unregistered church community, all of which have brought, and continue to bring, a new level of complexity to the relationship between China's official and unregistered church streams. These developments have resulted in a tense yet synergistic relationship between these two segments of the church.

The Communist Party of China is still officially atheist. As of today the TSPM has yet to acknowledge its role in the atrocities against non-cooperating pastors that took place in the 1950s and resulted in many spending

18. Mary Ma, interview with the author, August 15, 2014.
19. David Ro, interview with the author, August 12, 2014.

the following two decades or longer in prison or labor camp. Nevertheless religious policy of the past thirty years has stressed the positive contribution of religious believers to China's national reconstruction rather than the Marxian characterization of religion as the "opiate of the masses." Within this framework the TSPM's role has shifted from an anti-imperialist program of curtailing the church's influence to a focus on ensuring "normal" church development. The need to distance itself from its anti-imperialist past prompted the late Bishop Ding Guangxun (K.H. Ting), then head of the TSPM, to ask in 1987 whether it wouldn't be better to eliminate the TSPM altogether and entrust the work of China's official church to the newly created China Christian Council. (In the wake of the 1989 Tiananmen uprising, political reform ground to a halt and Ding's proposal was shelved.)

The leadership of the TSPM and China Christian Council at the national, provincial, and local levels is overlapping, if not completely identical; thus they are often referred to in Chinese as "the two associations" (*lianghui*). As the TSPM's sister organization, the China Christian Council resources the church with Bibles, pastoral training, literature, and other forms of support, all of which indirectly benefit the unregistered church as well. Not a few pastors trained in the *lianghui* system have left to serve the unregistered church yet still maintain their *lianghui* ties, thus enabling them to keep their unregistered church counterparts informed about impending policy changes that might affect them. In both the registered and unregistered communities, there is emerging a new generation of believers who are largely evangelical in conviction and generally apolitical, with little interest in perpetuating the kind of heated debates that characterized relations in the 1950s and 1980s. It is less common to hear unregistered church leaders refer to registered church leaders as political pawns or to hear registered church leaders call those in the unregistered church untrained peasants or criminals.[20]

More than a few of those in TSPM pulpits today grew up in house church families in the latter years of Mao's reign. As believers from both camps rub shoulders with one another in the city, old stereotypes break down. Meanwhile, most of those in the emerging urban professional church have ties to neither the TSPM nor the traditional house churches (although their sympathies would lie with the latter).

Significant tensions remain, however, not the least of which is the enduring question that has been at the center of opposition to the TSPM

20. M. D., interview with the author, July 4, 2014.

since its inception, namely, "Who is head of the church?" China's political structure puts the TSPM firmly under the control of the United Front Department, a branch of the Party responsible for supervising non-party elements in society. Its personnel appointment structure mirrors that of the Party's *nomenclatura* system. In this sense the TSPM's function is clearly political: to ensure the Party's ultimate control over the church. However, as a political organization directing church affairs, the TSPM occupies a very ambiguous position. In the words of Ding Guangxun, it is "like a church, but not a church; like a government organ, but not a government organ."[21]

As the *de facto* authority on theological orthodoxy, the *lianghui* has privileged status as a quasi-denominational structure in China's "post-denominational" church, a position that puts considerable power in the hands of *lianghui* leaders. Current regulations create a legal framework for the church that ultimately gives the government a strong hand in matters including leadership selection, assignments of pastors to churches, church decision making, setting quotas for baptisms, acquisition of property for church facilities, relationships with Christian groups overseas, and evangelistic activities.[22] As in the unregistered church, believers operating within the TSPM structure have shown remarkable creativity in the face of these restrictions, not only in maintaining church activities but also expanding the church's reach. Their sensitive position vis-à-vis the government and the believers has, in the words of one observer, "forced them to think more" about how to be faithful to their calling while still satisfying official demands.[23]

With urbanization, the continued numerical growth of the church, and the emergence of a new generation of younger, more sophisticated and more cosmopolitan believers, the registered church faces serious capacity issues. Most registered churches are already filled to overflowing, but, with land at a premium, particularly in China's urban centers, the building of new churches is extremely rare. Culturally, the development of leadership and programs has lagged behind much of what has been taking place in the unregistered church, exacerbating the generational gap between older pastors and younger believers. One registered church pastor lamented, with a hint of bitterness in his voice, "People come to faith in the big church with the giant cross on top, hear the gospel, and get baptized. Then within a couple

21. Sun, "Why We Don't Join."

22. Ibid.

23. Y. M., interview with the author, July 8, 2014.

years they leave and join the unregistered church."[24] Young people in the official churches, including those who have gone to TSPM seminaries, have a hard time fitting in. They often end up starting their own groups as they feel there is no recognition of their gifts and calling in the official church. Visionary believers in the registered church who want to start ministry among the needy in their community may find their efforts thwarted by pastors who fear that such projects might drain resources away from the church.[25]

Younger leaders within the TSPM umbrella who see the need for change are able to push the envelope with at least some assurance of official cover. The unregistered churches have no such guarantee unless they are willing to come into the TSPM system, the *de facto* requirement for official registration in most places. This puts the two on very different footing and creates the current untenable situation in which the government tolerates the proliferation of unregistered churches but refuses to grant them legal status. In the eyes of unregistered church leaders, the TSPM has no legitimate authority over the church.[26] Although most urban unregistered church leaders would be open to working with the registered church "at the right time and under the right circumstances," for now they see the TSPM-affiliated churches as being "under slavery" as long as the TSPM is under the control of the Party.[27]

Differences exist, however, concerning when "the right time" might be. In cases where an amicable relationship exists between unregistered and TSPM church leaders in a city, the unregistered church may agree to seek legal status as a registered meeting point of the local TSPM church in return for the freedom to basically continue running the church as they have been doing. Other unregistered church leaders, however, would look on this arrangement as "selling out." Differences also exist within the unregistered church around how far to go in opposing government restrictions and defending the church's right to exist.

In the case of Shouwang Church, which was forced out of its rented premises in 2011, the decision to meet outdoors for worship was seen by church leaders as a form of civil disobedience, which they resorted to after all other attempts to reach a workable arrangement with the government had failed. Senior leaders in the church also saw this move as a historical

24. Andrew Kaiser, interview with the author, July 22, 2014.
25. Ibid.
26. Lin, "House Churches' Understanding."
27. David Ro, interview with the author, August 12, 2014.

turning point, not only for Shouwang, but for the unregistered church at large, with Shouwang leading the way in the struggle for official recognition. Not all inside the church agreed, however, that the church had been called to engage in this kind of political action. Eventually several hundred members as well as key staff left for other churches.

TOWARD DENOMINATIONAL STRUCTURES

Although the church in China is known as being "post-denominational," since denominational structures ceased to exist following the formation of the TSPM in 1950, in reality the organizational and doctrinal influence of early 20th century indigenous movements has been significant, both through the endurance of groups such as Watchman Nee's "Little Flock" and through the formation of some of the larger rural networks that have roots in movements such as the True Jesus Church and the Jesus Family.[28] One may also argue that the TSPM-affiliated churches and some traditional urban churches have maintained much of the ecclesiastical flavor—through their hymns, liturgies, style of worship, and offices within the church, for example—of the Western denominations and mission societies that largely dominated in China before 1949. The China Christian Council is not a denomination, but the *lianghui* does, in fact, fulfill a number of denominational functions through its process of qualifying and appointing pastors, its production of approved curriculum and liturgical resources, and its formulation of organizational protocols for churches.

In the past decade urban unregistered church leaders in particular have been exploring the biblical basis for denominational structures as well as their ability to address challenges currently facing the church. Unregistered church leaders also see the move toward denominations as enhancing the legitimacy of the church, making it harder for government or official church critics to attack them for being unorganized and increasing the church's attractiveness to an increasingly sophisticated and demanding urban population. As discussed in chapter two, the strongest denominational advocates to date have been those church leaders in China who subscribe to the Reformed tradition.

One urban church leader commented that, without denominations, churches are "captive" to individual leaders, subject to individual whims, indifferent to others' concerns, vulnerable to heresies, and have a narrow

28. Xi, *Redeemed by Fire*, 215–20.

understanding of God's kingdom.[29] The phenomenon of "strongman" leaders ruling the church in a dictatorial fashion suggests the need for the accountability that comes with a plurality of leaders who meet a minimum set of qualifications and are duly installed through a process of ordination. Leaders can be quite isolated from one another and traditionally very top-down in dealing with their congregations. Denominational structures provide a mechanism whereby leaders become answerable to others within the church. Where leadership failure or abuses occur there would be the means to address the errant behavior, care for those who may have been affected, and seek the restoration of the leader.

Denominational structures can also help to address the need for orthodox teaching. Unregistered churches have, over the years, given birth to myriad cults and heresies due to a lack of solid biblical teaching. A coherent theological framework, such as that offered by the Reformed tradition, addresses this shortcoming. In the absence of strong teaching for children—a need now being recognized as acute in the unregistered church, a catechism can give families and church leaders a framework for family Christian education. Church government has traditionally not been a strong point of the unregistered church, as the emphasis has been on evangelism, not on church administration. Here again, denominational structures and procedures provide proven answers to questions about how to manage the affairs of the church.

Looking beyond the individual congregation to the larger Christian community, denominational identification and structures could allow churches to go further than simply relating informally via pastors fellowships, alumni associations, or joint projects and to collaborate in a more intentional, long-term fashion, with mutual accountability between them. Within the church at large, denominations potentially allow believers to stand together as one and still maintain their unique differences.[30] Strengthened inter-church relationships would bolster the church's position vis-à-vis the government. In cases where the church is accused of cult activity, for example, denominational leaders could make a case for the church's orthodoxy. In the future, should there be a thaw in official relations with the unregistered church, the unity that comes with denominational structures could help bolster the church's case for being allowed to exist legally apart from aligning with the TSPM. On the other hand, in the current situation

---

29. Gao, "Why China Needs Presbyterianism."

30. Andrew Kaiser, interview with the author, July 22, 2014.

the development of city or regional presbyteries comprising a new system that could potentially rival the TSPM's monopoly position would undoubtedly be viewed as a threat by the government.

Urban believers see denominational structures as enhancing the church's position in society by, for example, providing a clear, recognizable identity ("branding" in marketing parlance), thus helping an uninformed or skeptical public to understand the nature and purpose of the church. Similarly, some see a cohesive structure as appealing to China's urban intellectuals, who have tended to view churches as scattered collections of disaffected, superstitious and largely uneducated people with questionable Western connections and nothing of substance to offer society. In this regard, identifiable structures led by well-educated believers, many of whom hold responsible positions in society, would provide the church with legitimacy in intellectual circles, particularly vis-à-vis the competing "schools" that are currently debating China's future cultural and spiritual direction.

Others, however, would suggest it is inappropriate for foreign denominational structures and traditions to be adopted as the yardstick for measuring every aspect of church life. If something in the Chinese church experience seems in error or does not fit, it can too easily be labeled as wrong, without examining both the old and the new critically in the light of Scripture. The current examination of the role of denominations in China today is necessary as leaders seek to shore up areas in the church that have been lacking. Nonetheless, unless this exploration is conducted in a spirit of humility, it is possible that well-meaning attempts to address very real needs in China's church could unwittingly turn into lines drawn in the sand, accentuating divisions rather than inviting constructive dialog with those of different traditions.

A CHURCH AT THE CROSSROADS

During the past century China's church has weathered, *inter alia*, the fundamentalist/modernist debates of the 1920s; power struggles between indigenous Christian leaders and their missionary counterparts, civil war between the Nationalists and Communists; attacks within the church by the TSPM leadership against those who refused to join the movement; the divisive campaigns, counter campaigns, and personal vendettas of the Cultural Revolution, which scarred an entire nation; and, since the early 1980s, ongoing TSPM/house church tensions. The rise of a new generation of church leaders in China's cities, who personally have been unencumbered by much of this difficult history, sounds a hopeful note that perhaps it is the dawning of a new day for China's church. New vistas of opportunity for the church, requiring a deeper level of cooperation, loom on the horizon. Urbanization has created conditions in which this cooperation is more likely to take place.

Having moved beyond survival mode to a place where it is now confronting questions about its future role, China's church is at a crossroads. Its current and future leaders cannot ignore the legacy of the past century, but neither do they need to be bound by it. Reflecting on where the church has been spiritually, organizationally, and politically offers lessons that can speak to many of the issues that the church faces today. Faced with both the practical and spiritual necessity of unity, these leaders now have the opportunity to build internal structures that will enable believers to show mutual respect for differences while still embracing the broadly held tenets of the faith. Doing so with credibility will require that they first learn to demonstrate personal forbearance in dealing with their peers, particularly where theological differences exist. By building unity internally the church will be better equipped to deal with outward threats to its unity, including the religious policy and control structures that continue to stand in the way of Christians' efforts "to be one."

8

Testing the Limits

"But the word of God is not chained!"[1]

THIS STUDY BEGAN WITH the thesis that, as China urbanizes, its Christians are more concerned with the challenges posed by urbanization—both to the internal working of the church as well as in the outworking of its mission in society—than with the threat of an oppressive Chinese party-state. In other words, their most pressing interests are more practical than political. While the foregoing discussion has shown evidence of this in the life of the Chinese church today, the political realities facing China's Christians cannot be ignored. Should Christians in China continue along their present trajectory, these political realities will likely become of greater concern in the days to come.

As urban believers have sought to work out the implications of their faith within China's rapidly changing social environment, this journey has taken them into areas that previously had not had a significant Christian presence. In these various spheres they have been extending the meaning of Christian faith in China beyond merely a pietistic, inward-looking devotion and toward an outward-focused, mission-driven expression of their faith commitment. In this current process, China's urban Christians cannot avoid running up against the political limits imposed by the Chinese party-state. In some cases, this resistance may be stiffer than others; however, as Christians advance into areas where they heretofore had not been active,

1. 2 Timothy 2:9.

they inevitably confront a regime that is either unprepared or unwilling to allow them to progress further.

THE LIMITS OF FREEDOM

Article 36 of the Chinese Constitution guarantees freedom of religious belief but offers little protection to the practice of that belief. Although the Constitution forbids discrimination on the basis of religion and mandates that the state protect "normal" religious activities, it also stipulates that religious activities shall not disrupt public order, endanger the health of citizens, or interfere with the state's educational system; nor should religious activities be under the control of foreign entities. Clearly the guarantee of religious freedom is conditioned, firstly upon whatever definition of "normal" activities the state wishes to invoke, and secondly upon the state's interest in guiding social and individual development, including the exclusion of foreign religious influence.

According to Zhang Yushuang of the China University of Political Science and Law, making sense of Article 36 requires viewing it through two lenses, one historical, the other political. Zhang points to three historical factors that have conditioned the Chinese state's view toward religion. Firstly, China's traditional Confucian ideology, a kind of theocracy in Zhang's view, placed all religion under state domination. Secondly, successive regimes from the Tang Dynasty onward have all followed suit and required religious organizations to register with the state, which has assumed the right to monitor and to intervene in religious affairs. China's current religious control mechanisms are thus not an anomaly but have longstanding political precedent. Finally, where the Christian faith is concerned, the Opium War signaled the beginning of a clash between the Chinese state and Christianity in particular, which came to be seen as a foreign religion directly threatening Chinese culture and thought. These factors have all contributed to the current regime's stance on religion as something to be allowed only within limits. They also shed light on the state's concern, voiced at the end of Article 36, that religion could again become a tool in the hands of foreign forces intent on destabilizing China.

The political lens comes into focus as one examines the Constitution's Preamble and General Principles, which, according to Zhang, establish a clear hierarchy of values. At the top is the preeminence of the Chinese Communist Party, followed by socialism, democratic centralism, China's modern socialist construction, and, finally, the protection of individual rights. "To sum up," Zhang says, "the wide variety of freedoms protected in the Constitution have less to do with human dignity or intrinsic value of life than with the collective morality needed for the accumulation of national material wealth."[2] Viewed within this hierarchy, religion is not protected as an inalienable right in the Western sense. Rather, religion is valuable only to the extent that it serves the larger goal of socialist construction under the leadership of the Party. Hence, according to Zhang, the stipulation that the state will protect only "normal" religious activities, leaving it up to administrative authorities to define "normal" according to the needs and requirements of the state.

Furthermore, the freedom of religious belief enshrined in the Constitution is not actively protected by the Chinese legal system, which is itself subservient to the Communist Party of China. Rather, the responsibility for deciding how and when it will be protected is delegated to administrative organs (such as the State Administration for Religious Affairs and the Ministry of Public Security), leaving no legal recourse for believers who find their fundamental rights have been infringed.

CONTINUING CLASS STRUGGLE

The lack of legal protection and the bias toward "controlling" religion evidenced in China's Constitution point to an institutionalized discrimination against religion based in an underlying assumption that religion is a problem, rather than a positive force in society. As Zhang Shoudong of the University of Politics and Law in Beijing points out, the Party's stance toward religion has been rooted in the concept of class struggle since the founding the Party. Although current official discussions of religion do not deal with religion in these terms, the notion of class struggle still underpins the Party's ideas about religion and how it is to be dealt with. Religious groups are seen as posing a particular threat to national security and social harmony and are thus singled out among other groups in society as needing special regulation. Those within the officially sanctioned religious bodies (in the case of Protestant Christians, the TSPM/CCC) are treated as objects of an imposed "church-state harmony," while unregistered groups, viewed as the enemy, are essentially objects of class struggle. In the words of Zhang Shoudong,

2. Zhang, "Political Constitution," 90.

At the same time that state-religion harmony is being promoted, the model of class struggle still persists. I think that it is more accurate to describe official church-state relations today as being a combination of state-church harmony and class struggle. It claims that, similar to other citizens, religious citizens enjoy the same political, economic, social and cultural rights. Yet, it emphasizes that religion must correspond with the socialist society and that it has special features. In the final analysis, the goal of state-church relations remains guiding religion to conform to the socialist society, assimilating it into the official ideology, with the corresponding loss of its salient features.[3]

This negative orientation toward religion manifests itself in the lives of Chinese Christians in numerous ways, creating obstacles to their fully realizing a vision of the Christian community playing a multi-faceted role in China's urban society. By delimiting religion's sphere of influence (as seen in the Constitutional references to education and to "normal" religious activities, for example), current policy circumscribes the believer's role. Although China's Christians have found ways to become creatively involved in various sectors of society, in each of these areas the Party retains the prerogative to tell Christians how far they can go. Their push into areas such as education or social media may be unprecedented, but China's urban believers have no guarantees that they will not be forced to retreat in the future.

A case in point is the Zhejiang Provincial government's backlash against rampant church construction in Wenzhou, highlighted by the bulldozing of Sanjiang Church in April 2014 and the removal of hundreds of crosses from church buildings in Wenzhou and elsewhere in the province. Using the pretense of building violations (as many of the structures, including Sanjiang Church, had exceeded what had been allowed in their respective building permits), the provincial government unleashed a three-year campaign culminating in new legislation containing precise regulations on the size and location of religious buildings and the size and placement of crosses.[4] The fact that the campaign has mostly targeted registered churches further highlights the church's precarious legal status. Until the Zhejiang regulations, there had been no clear limits set on the display of Christian symbols on churches—the mark of the church's identity in the public sphere. Thus the provincial government becomes the arbiter of how public a presence the church is allowed to have. Whether Zhejiang will become a

3. Zhang, "The Relationship."
4. Forsythe, "Chinese Province."

test case for other localities or even for national-level regulations remains to be seen.

In response to the government's call for comments on the draft legislation, one Zhejiang pastor wrote a lengthy letter questioning the scientific and aesthetic basis for the restrictions, why the regulations apply only to Christian places of worship, and why the standards for Protestant and Catholic churches are different. The letter closes with an appeal for rationality and fairness in dealing with religion:

> This writer is willing to say that the majority of colleagues in the religious community support the leadership of the Party, they take the lead in observing the law, they strive to be of one mind, and they contribute their own energy to building a prosperous society. At the same time, this writer also looks forward to a time when the relevant government departments can approach religion rationally, treat religion favorably, and genuinely respect other people's religious beliefs. Therefore, in order to continue to preserve excellent conditions for religious harmony, I call for greater effort to improve the "Building Regulations." Or, when conditions are ripe, to reissue a draft "Regulations" that the religious community can truly take to heart, that comforts the hearts of religious believers, and increases the power of the "Chinese Dream!"[5]

DRAWING THE LINE

In the publishing sector, although more than a thousand Christian titles have made their way legally into Chinese bookstores, there is a general understanding among China's 663 sanctioned publishing houses that religious—in particular Christian—content is sensitive. It is up to government censors to indicate where the line of acceptability lies. Christian authors' forays into mainstream publishing are thus possible, but by no means guaranteed. The cost, both financially and in terms of risk, are high, effectively limiting what could otherwise be a thriving industry.

China's online Christian community, meanwhile, continues to enjoy the relative lack of restrictions on the Internet, a new medium where regulations have not yet caught up with reality. As in the case of the Wenzhou churches, it is possible that authorities may at some point decide the Christian online presence is too pervasive. In the absence of legal definition, there

5. "Now, about Those 'Cross Size' Regulations."

is no clear line indicating how much and what kind of Christian activity is acceptable. In the current political climate, should such legislation appear, the line would likely tend toward greater restriction.

The party-state's assumption that religion is a negative force in society also prevents Christians from formally organizing for the purpose of furthering many of the activities enumerated in the previous chapters. In this way China's Christians are effectively denied the Constitutional guarantee of freedom of association for all Chinese citizens. As part of the Party's united front strategy, all non-party elements in society must be supervised by officially sanctioned organizations designed to enforce the will of the Party at the grassroots level. For China's Christians, apart from the Party-controlled TSPM, there can be no other officially recognized organization. Although some voices within the Party have, at various times, encouraged the official recognition of Christian bodies outside the TSPM, at the time of this writing no such provision exists.

Some groups have come into being, such as a nationwide network of Christian counselors or an association of Christian-run schools, and these play a connecting function among individual believers or groups. However, due to the Party's concern about any social organization it does not directly control, these associations must maintain a low profile. Given that the majority of China's Christians are outside the TSPM structure, their inability to collaborate places severe restrictions on the church's capacity to train leaders, distribute resources, share knowledge, or hold leaders accountable within the larger Christian community. As denominationalism takes hold in parts of the church, individual congregations will form more unofficial linkages between themselves and with entities such as unofficial seminaries and mission sending bodies. Nevertheless the inability of churches and other Christian-run entities to openly affiliate will continue to hamper the effectiveness of such linkages and impede the healthy development of the church.

Efforts to organize for the purpose of interfacing with counterparts outside China also meet with resistance, as evidenced by the official response when some 200 unregistered church leaders attempted to join Capetown 2010, the international congress in South Africa hosted by the Lausanne Committee on World Evangelization, an interdenominational Christian body. Apart from a few participants who were already outside of China for other reasons, China was essentially absent from this historic international gathering. Neither Lausanne nor the World Evangelical

Alliance, an international association of evangelical fellowships representing more than 100 nations, have been able to solve the conundrum of relating to churches in China that are forbidden to present a united face to the outside world while also relating to the TSPM, an official entity that considers itself the sole representative of China's Christians. The World Council of Churches has, since China's opening, related solely to the TSPM. As a result of the restrictions on China's Christians engaging formally in forums such as Lausanne, Christians in China are deprived of valuable interaction with the global church, which in turn loses the opportunity to learn from the experience of the church in China.

NO LEGAL STATUS

Restrictions on formal organization are directly linked to the church's lack of legal status. Practical concerns currently facing the urban church, such as the question of who should hold the lease or deed to an unregistered church property, are likewise symptoms of this larger issue. Attempts by unregistered churches, such as Shouwang Church in Beijing, to attain legal status have thus far been thwarted by authorities, who essentially contend that current regulations do not allow churches any legal position outside the TSPM framework. Zhang Shoudong describes as a "double veto" the requirements of, respectively, the State Administration of Religious Affairs and the Department of Civil Affairs, which, taken together, effectively require any church seeking registration to be certified by the TSPM, which would not likely be forthcoming since the leaders of the church in question would not have been trained in the TSPM system. In the case of Shouwang, the church's application to the Department of Civil Affairs stalled after the District Bureau of Religious Affairs rejected it on the grounds that Shouwang's leaders were not certified by the TSPM; thus it lacked professional personnel with proper qualifications to run the church.[6]

The church's lack of legal status is increasingly problematic as more Christians undertake various types of social service. Without the ability to open bank accounts, acquire facilities, hire staff, and process donations, unregistered Christian groups desiring to address social needs are hindered from becoming involved in a sustainable manner. Some have managed to carry out their work under the guise of a business or consulting firm. Launching a registered NGO in China is a difficult endeavor given the

6. Zhang, "The Relationship."

party-state's ambivalence, discussed in chapter five, toward the nonprofit sector. For Christians, the difficulty is compounded by the government's inherent mistrust of religious groups, particularly if the believers in question belong to an unregistered church that is already under surveillance by local authorities.

Christians' lack of legal status not only impinges upon their ability to carry out activities motivated by their Christian commitment; it also precludes most from meaningful involvement in China's political life. Some TSPM officials and pastors sit on China's legislature, the National People's Congress, or on provincial People's Congresses. Others are members of the political consultative conferences (intended as connecting points between the Party and non-party elements in society) at various levels. However, for most unregistered church leaders such a position would be out of the question, the exception being those selected to serve on the basis of their academic or professional credentials or their membership in one of China's ethnic minority groups. It goes without saying that the Party itself and the military, both of which forbid their members from believing in religion, are officially closed to China's Christians (although some believers will admit privately that they are Party members).

OFF-LIMITS

Finally, the party-state's institutionalized discrimination against religion results in Christians being specifically excluded from areas where their involvement might pose a threat to Party control. Despite decades of liberalization, China's Leninist structure requires that authority over all spheres of society rest ultimately with the Communist Party. Referring again to China's Constitution, religious believers are expressly not allowed to "interfere with the education system of the State."[7] That this prohibition is enshrined in the Constitution suggests how seriously the party-state takes its role as the nation's sole educational authority. This clause also belies the assumption that religious groups in China might have other designs for the education of their members and their children, which could run counter to the intentions of the Party.

As discussed in chapter four, this prohibition has not prevented Christians from stepping into the educational arena; yet their involvement in this sensitive area, although courageous, remains tentative, largely outside

7. *Constitution of the People's Republic of China*, art. 36.

the realm of legality. While private schools have become a growth industry in urban China, with parents willing to hand over large sums to secure coveted school places in prestigious institutions, particularly those with international connections, the high cost of entry, as well as tight restrictions on who can start a school and what can be taught in the classroom, have prevented Christians from making significant inroads into legal private education. Given the vision of many Christian educators to see believers play more of a role in this sphere, and given the demand from parents for an alternative to the state system, Christians in China may be expected to continue to devise new avenues for involvement in the hope that education reform will loosen the state's grip on this politically sensitive area. Unless and until that happens, the drive to establish Christian education in China will continue to be a stiff uphill battle. As a domain that has historically been under state control and at various times has constituted an ideological battlefield, education provides a particularly salient example of how the party-state's need to control precludes meaningful Christian involvement on a significant scale.

A GRAY AREA

As pointed out at the beginning of this book, the central issue for China's Christians has shifted from freedom of belief to freedom of association. China's current constitution protects individual faith; except for party members and those in the military, possessing religious belief does not constitute an offense against the state. The outworking of that faith, however, is another story. Outside of a tightly constructed box intended to contain the influence of religion, exercising one's faith publicly, particularly in concert with other believers, can take one beyond the protected area of "normal" religious activity and into a gray area in which one's behavior may or may not be allowed. Although this gray area has grown significantly in recent decades, creating the space for China's Christians to explore the outworking of their faith in new ways, the boundaries remain. China's urban context has served to highlight both the opportunities for creative Christian participation in a variety of social spheres as well as the limits on those activities.

9

Conclusion

"For here we have no continuing city,
but we seek the one to come."[1]

ALONG WITH THE MASSIVE urbanization that has forever reshaped the geographical and social landscape of China, the Christian church in China has itself undergone a major transformation. From a largely rural, peasant-led movement in the 1980s, the church is now very much an urban phenomenon.

The relative social space and position afforded by the city represent, for the church, a double-edged sword. The stature, influence, and resources of the urban church, whether registered or unregistered, could be both a boon and a bane to the future of the Christian faith in an urbanized China. Extensive use of the Internet and social media, particularly involving believers who are well-known figures in the society, as well as ventures into areas such as education, social service, philanthropy, publishing, entrepreneurship, and community leadership will raise the profile of Christians and provide new avenues for extending the church's reach. The church's growing intellectual and financial resources will undergird the development of a new "Christian infrastructure."

On the other hand, the church's own success could become a liability if building this infrastructure becomes an end in itself and competition for

1. Hebrews 13:14.

people, resources, and influence serve to fragment the church. Furthermore, should the Christian community's growing influence be seen as a threat by China's political and cultural elites, there could come a backlash in the form of new restrictions aimed at limiting Christians' penetration into the culture.

While deeply committed to having an influence on the life of their cities, China's Christians are able to face opposition precisely because their hope is set, not on the future of the temporal urban community to which they currently belong, but ultimately on the promise of a city yet to come. Some in China's urban church will feel called to take a stand against the political forces that obstruct the church's development. Some, such as Christian human rights lawyers or believers who are on the forefront of extending China's NGO sector, point out injustices, advocate on behalf of the oppressed, and engage their government as they fight for social change. Many more of China's Christians, obeying the biblical injunction to be "salt and light," will, on a personal level, bring change in their own workplaces, communities and families.

Yet they know that their vision for urban China is but a faint reflection of their vision of an eternal city. They know that this vision will not be fulfilled on this earth, whether in their lifetimes or in some future era. Still the pattern of this city to come, an ideal set forth in the image of the kingdom of God as portrayed in Scripture, inspires them to seek the attributes of this kingdom in their current environment. Knowing that this vision will ultimately be fulfilled only in eternity, they believe that the fruit of their labors in the earthly city will also only be made clear when seen from an eternal perspective. It is their humble acknowledgment of their role—limited yet having eternal importance—that enables them to persevere in building the city on a hill even as they set their eyes on a city yet to come.

Bibliography

"A Beijing Pastor Discusses the Vision of His Urban Church (I)." http://www.chinasource. org/resource-library/chinese-church-voices/a-beijing-pastor-discusses-the-vision-of-his-urban-church-i.

Aikman, David. *Jesus in Beijing: How Christianity is Transforming China and Changing the Global Balance of Power.* Washington, DC: Regnery, 2003.

Andrews-Speed, Philip. "China's Energy Policymaking Processes and Their Consequences." In *China's Energy Crossroads: Forging a New Energy and Environmental Balance,* edited by Philip Andrews-Speed, Mikkal E Herberg and Zhidong Li. *NBR Special Report* 47 (November 2014) 1–17.

"Another Baby Slaughtered: Where Is God?" http://www.chinasource.org/resource-library/chinese-church-voices/another-baby-slaughtered-where-is-god.

"Are Chinese Men Good Enough for Chinese Women?" http://www.echinacities.com/china-media/Are-Chinese-Men-Good-Enough-for-Chinese-Women/.

Atsmon, Yuvai, and Max Magni. "Meet the Chinese consumer of 2020." *McKinsey Quarterly* (March 2012), http://www.mckinsey.com/insights/asia-pacific/meet_the_chinese_consumer_of_2020/.

Barbalas, Michael, interview with the author, June 29, 2014.

Baugus, Bruce P. "China, Church Development, and Presbyterianism." In *China's Reforming Churches*, edited by Bruce P. Baugus, 1–23. Grand Rapids: Reformation Heritage Books, 2014.

Bays, Daniel H. *A New History of Christianity in China.* Chichester, UK: Wiley-Blackwell, 2012.

"Building a Chinese Church Culture." http://www.chinasource.org/resource-library/chinese-church-voices/building-a-chinese-church-culture/.

"Building the Dream." *The Economist* (April 29, 2014). http://www.economist.com/news/special-report/21600797-2030-chinese-cities-will-be-home-about-1-billion-people-getting-urban-china-work/.

C. C. Interview with the author, July 15, 2014.

Cao, Nanlai. *Constructing China's Jerusalem: Christians, Power and Place in Contemporary Wenzhou.* Stanford: Stanford University Press, 2011.

Chan, Kim-Kwong. Interview with the author, July 4, 2014.

Chang, Rachel. "More Unwed Couples Living Together." http://news.asiaone.com/news/diva/more-unwed-couples-china-living-together/.

Chen, Fielding. "Life Expectancy." *Bloomberg Brief* (May 15, 2015) 9. http://www.bloombergbriefs.com/content/uploads/sites/2/2015/05/China-Smog.pdf/.

Chen, Liang. "Between God and Mammon." *Global Times* (February 27, 2014). http://www.globaltimes.cn/content/845019.shtml.

Cheng, John. "China's Christian Education Today." *ChinaSource Quarterly* 16.2 (2014). http://www.chinasource.org/resource-library/articles/chinas-christian-education-today/.

"China to Speed Up Agri Modernization through Reforms, Innovations." *Xinhuanet* (Feb. 1, 2015). http://news.xinhuanet.com/english/china/2015-02/01/c_133962873.htm/.

"China's Smog War Seen Dooming Coal on 'Cheap but Dirty' Purge." *BloombergBusiness* (May 19, 2015). http://www.bloomberg.com/news/articles/2015-05-18/china-war-on-smog-seen-dooming-coal-amid-cheap-but-dirty-purge.

"Chinese Christian Dating Sites." http://www.chinasource.org/resource-library/chinese-church-voices/chinese-christian-dating-sites.

Chow, Alexander. "Calvinist Public Theology in Urban China Today." *International Journal of Public Theology* 8.2 (May 2014) 158–75.

"The Church Today." http://www.chinasource.org/resource-library/chinese-church-voices/the-church-today/.

Conkling, Timothy G. *Mobilized Merchants—Patriotic Martyrs: China's House Church Christians and the Politics of Cooperative Resistance*. CreateSpace Independent Publishing Platform, 2013.

"Constitution of the People's Republic of China." No pages. http://www.npc.gov.cn/englishnpc/Constitution/2007-11/15/content_1372964.htm.

"Cracks in the Atheist Edifice." *The Economist* (November 1, 2014). No pages. http://www.economist.com/news/briefing/21629218-rapid-spread-christianity-forcing-official-rethink-religion-cracks/.

Cresswell, Matthew. "What Future for the Lausanne Movement." *The Guardian*, Oct. 21, 2010. http://www.theguardian.com/commentisfree/belief/2010/oct/21/lausanne-movement/.

"Demolish! It's Just a Building!" http://www.chinasource.org/resource-library/chinese-church-voices/demolish-its-just-a-building/.

"Do Chinese Men and Women Deserve Each Other?" http://www.chinasource.org/blog/posts/do-chinese-men-and-women-deserve-each-other/.

"Don't Just be a Sunday Christian." http://www.chinasource.org/resource-library/chinese-church-voices/dont-just-be-a-sunday-christian.

Doyle, G. Wright. "Confucian Comeback: An Interview with Yang Fenggang." http://www.chinasource.org/resource-library/articles/confucian-comeback-an-interview-with-fenggang-yang/.

Economy, Elizabeth. "China's Environmental Future: The Power of the People." *McKinsey Quarterly* (June 2013). http://www.mckinsey.com/insights/asia-pacific/chinas_environmental_future_the_power_of_the_people?cid=china-eml-alt-mip-mck-oth-1306/.

"Enter the Chinese NGO." *The Economist* (April 12, 2014). http://www.economist.com/news/leaders/21600683-communist-party-giving-more-freedom-revolutionary-idea-enter-chinese-ngo/.

"Evangelism and Missions—the Future for the Chinese Church." http://www.chinasource.org/blog/posts/evangelism-and-missions-the-future-for-the-chinese-church.

Fällman, Fredrik. "Urge for Faith: Postmodern Beliefs among Urban Chinese." *ChinaSource Quarterly* 15.3 (September 2013). http://www.chinasource.org/resource-library/articles/urge-for-faith-postmodern-beliefs-among-urban-chinese/.

Forsythe, Michael. "Chinese Province Issues Draft Regulations on Church Crosses." *New York Times,* May 8, 2015, http://www.nytimes.com/2015/05/09/world/asia/china-church-crosses.html?_r=0.

"Full Text of the Oxford Consensus 2013." http://sinosphere.blogs.nytimes.com/2013/10/18/full-text-of-the-oxford-consensus-2013/.

Fulton, Brent. "Healthy Partnering: A Chinese Perspective." http://www.chinasource.org/resource-library/articles/healthy-partnering-a-chinese-perspective/.

———. "In Their Own Words: Perceived Challenges of Christians in China." In *China's Reforming Churches: Mission, Polity, and Ministry in the Next Christendom,* edited by Bruce P. Baugus, 99–117. Grand Rapids: Reformation Heritage Books, 2014.

Gao, Zheng. "Why China Needs Presbyterianism." Presbyterianism in China conference, Washington, DC, January 4, 2013.

"Gender Imbalance in China." http://www.allgirlsallowed.org/gender-imbalance-china-statistics/.

Goossaert, Vincent, and David A. Palmer, *The Religious Question in Modern China.* Chicago: University of Chicago Press, 2011.

Herberg, Mikkal E. "China's Search for Oil and Gas Security: Prospect and Implications." In *China's Energy Crossroads: Forging a New Energy and Environmental Balance,* edited by Philip Andrews-Speed, Mikkal E Herberg and Zhidong Li. *NBR Special Report* 47 (November 2014) 19–27.

Hopwood, Gary. Interview with the author, July 2, 2014.

Hornemann, Magda. "China: Weibo and Advancing Freedom of Religion or Belief." http://www.forum18.org/archive.php?article_id=1771.

Hsu, Promise. Interview with the author, October 9, 2014.

———. "Why Beijing's Largest House Church Refuses to Stop Meeting Outdoors." *Christianity Today* (April 26, 2011). http://www.christianitytoday.com/ct/2011/aprilweb-only/beijinghousechurch.html/.

Huang, Caroline. Interview with the author, July 16, 2014.

Huang, Lei. "A Beautiful Testimony of the Lord's Love in China (Zhu Ai Zai Zhongguo de Mei Hao Jianzheng)." *Great Commission Bi-Monthly* (June 2014) 12–15.

Huang, Yasheng. "China's great rebalancing: Promise and peril." *McKinsey Quarterly* (June 2013). http://www.mckinsey.com/insights/asia-pacific/chinas_great_rebalancing_promise_and_peril/.

Huo, Shui. "Two Transformations: The Future of Christianity in China." *ChinaSource Quarterly* 13, no. 3 (September 2011). http://www.chinasource.org/resource-library/articles/two-transformations-the-future-of-christianity-in-china/.

"The Institute." http://www.pacilution.com/english/ShowArticle.asp?ArticleID=3087.

"Interview with a Reformed Church Pastor (2)." http://www.chinasource.org/resource-library/chinese-church-voices/interview-with-a-reformed-church-pastor-2/.

J. G. "Marriage in China: Guilt Tripped." *The Economist* (May 7, 2014). http://www.economist.com/blogs/analects/2014/03/marriage-china/.

J. H. Interview with the author, July 22, 2014.

Jin, Mingri. "Pastor Jin on the Church and Social Responsibility." http://www.chinasource.org/blog/posts/pastor-jin-on-the-church-and-social-responsibility/.

Johnson, Ian. "Q&A: Yang Fenggang on the 'Oxford Consensus' and Public Trust in China." http://sinosphere.blogs.nytimes.com/2013/10/18/q-a-yang-fenggang-on-the-oxford-consensus-and-public-trust-in-china/?_r=0/.

Kaiser, Andrew. Interview with the author, July 22, 2014.

Kam, Yidu. Interview with the author, July 21, 2014.

Kim, Enoch. Interview with the author November 22, 2014.

Lambert, Tony. *China's Christian Millions*. Oxford: Monarch Books, 2006.

L. D. Interview with the author, July 7, 2014.

L. J. Interview with the author, January 22, 2014.

L. W. Interview with the author, July 9, 2014.

Lee, Eric. "Five Profound Mentoring Needs in China." *ChinaSource Quarterly* 16.3 (October 2014). http://www.chinasource.org/resource-library/articles/five-profound-mentoring-needs-in-china/.

Li, Dong. Interview with the author, October 3, 2013.

Liao, Yiwu. *God is Red: The Secret Story of how Christianity Survived and Flourished in Communist China*. New York: HarperCollins, 2011.

Lin, Gang. "The House Churches' Understanding of the Three-Self Church, Chinese Government and Themselves." http://pacilution.com/english/ShowArticle.asp?ArticleID=3119.

Liu, Dong. "Estranged Brethren." *Global Times* (October 10, 2013). http://www.globaltimes.cn/content/816929.shtml.

Liu, Peng. "The Achilles' Heel of China's Rise: Belief." http://www.pacilution.com/english/ShowArticle.asp?ArticleID=3076.

Liu, Tongsu, and Wang, Yi. *Guankan Zhongguo Chengshi Jiating Jiaohui*. Taipei: Christian Arts Press, 2012.

Lu, Angel. Interview with the author, October 31, 2014.

Lu, Jun. "Purdue Symposium 2014: Religious Freedom and Chinese Society: A Symposium of Case Analysis." https://www.purdue.edu/crcs/events/purdue-symposium/purdue-symposium-2014/.

Lui, Otto. Interview with the author, July 14, 2014.

M. D. Interview with the author, July 4, 2014.

Ma, Li, and Jin Li. "Remaking the Civic Space: The Rise of Unregistered Protestantism and Civic Engagement in Urban China." In *Christianity in Chinese Public Life: Religion, Society, and the Rule of Law*, edited by Joel A. Carpenter and Kevin R. den Dulk, 11–28. New York: Palgrave Macmillan, 2014.

Ma, Mary. Interview with the author, August 15, 2014.

Moll, Rob. "Great Leap Forward." *Christianity Today* (May 2008) 22–33.

"Now, about Those 'Cross Size' Regulations." http://www.chinasource.org/resource-library/chinese-church-voices/now-about-those-cross-size-regulations/.

"Overseas Missions: The Chinese Church in Action." http://www.chinasource.org/blog/posts/overseas-missions-the-chinese-church-in-action/.

Patton, Dominique. "More than 40 percent of China's Arable Land Degraded: Xinhua." http://www.reuters.com/article/2014/11/04/us-china-soil-idUSKBN0I0Y720141104/.

Philips, Tom. "Beijing Urged to Respect Religious Freedom amidst 'Anti-Church' Crackdown." *The Telegraph* (May 14, 2014). http://www.telegraph.co.uk/news/worldnews/asia/china/10829581/Beijing-urged-to-respect-religious-freedom-amid-anti-church-crackdown.html/.

Pinghuang, Xing. "Five Major Challenges Facing the Chinese Church." http://www.chinasource.org/resource-library/chinese-church-voices/five-major-challenges-facing-the-church/.

Pittman, Joann. "China's Online Christian Community." http://www.chinasource.org/resource-library/articles/chinas-online-christian-community.

Platt, John R. "China's Wealthy Are Banking on Extinction." http://www.takepart.com/feature/2015/03/24/china-endangered-species-banking-extinction-poaching-elephants-tigers-rhinos/.

"The Preach Everywhere Gospel Band." http://www.chinasource.org/resource-library/chinese-church-voices/the-preach-everywhere-gospel-band.

"Protestantism and the Future of China." http://www.chinasource.org/resource-library/chinese-church-voices/protestantism-and-the-future-of-china/.

"Reflections on Worship." http://www.chinasource.org/blog/posts/reflections-on-worship/.

Ro, David. Interview with the author, August 12, 2014.

Rolland, Nadège. "Chinas' New Silk Road." http://www.nbr.org/research/activity.aspx?id=531.

"Seoul Commitment." http://ccsm.amccsm.org/news/prayer/pu-171/.

Shobert, Benjamin A. "Senior Care in China: Challenges and Opportunities," China Business Review (April 1, 2012), www.chinabusinessreview.com.

———. "The Key Drivers of China's Environmental Policies." In *China's Energy Crossroads: Forging a New Energy and Environmental Balance,* edited by Philip Andrews-Speed, Mikkal E. Herberg and Zhidong Li. *NBR Special Report* 47 (November 2014) 47–59.

"Single Christians and Love: The Cost and Consequences of Adultery." http://www.chinasource.org/resource-library/chinese-church-voices/single-christians-and-love-the-cost-and-consequences-of-adultery.

Stark, Rodney, and Wang, Xiuhua. *A Star in the East: The Rise of Christianity in China.* West Conshohocken, PA: Templeton Press, 2015.

Stokols, Andrew. "China's Rural Urbanization: Road to Modernity or Ruin." https://prezi.com/—fe85p9l-d_/chinas-rural-urbanization/.

Sun, Yi. "Why We Don't Join the National TSPM." http://www.pacilution.com/english/ShowArticle.asp?ArticleID=3132/.

Swanson, Ana. "Why China Is Buying up Oklahoma and Texas." *The Washington Post,* June 3, 2015. http://www.washingtonpost.com/blogs/wonkblog/wp/2015/06/03/why-china-is-buying-up-oklahoma-and-texasma/.

Swells in the Middle Kingdom. "Calvinism on the Ground in China." http://www.chinasource.org/resource-library/from-the-west-courtyard/calvinism-on-the-ground-in-china/.

———. "The Tyranny of History and the China Dream." http://www.chinasource.org/blog/posts/the-tyranny-of-history-and-the-china-dream.

T. S. Interview with the author, August 13, 2014.

"Testimony of a Christian Artist." http://www.chinasource.org/resource-library/chinese-church-voices/testimony-of-a-christian-artist/print/.

Towson, Jeffrey, and Jonathan Woetzel. *The One Hour China Book: Two Peking University Professors Explain all of China Business in Six Short Stories.* Cayman Islands: Towson Group, LLC, 2013.

Van Wyck, Barry. "The Groundwater of 90% of China's Cities is Polluted." http://www.danwei.com/the-groundwater-of-90-of-chinese-cities-is-polluted/.

Wang, Jianguo. "New Wine and Old Skin, Part 1: Current Context of the Chinese Church." http://www.chinapartnership.org/2014/10/new-wine-and-old-skin-part-i-current-context-of-the-chinese-church/.

W. E. Interview with the author, July 13, 2014.

Bibliography

"The Wenzhou Church Reborn from the Ashes." http://www.chinasource.org/resource-library/chinese-church-voices/the-wenzhou-church-reborn-from-the-ashes.

"Why Marriage Retreats Are Important." http://www.chinasource.org/resource-library/chinese-church-voices/why-marriage-retreats-are-important.

Wielander, Gerda. "Researching Chinese Christianity: (Mis)conceptions and revelations." *The China Story* (January 8, 2014). https://www.thechinastory.org/2014/01/researching-chinese-christianity-misconceptions-and-revelations/.

———. *Christian Values in Communist China*. New York: Routledge, 2013.

Wilberforce, William. *A Practical View of Christianity*. Peabody, MA: Hendirckson, 1996.

W. T. Interview with the author, July 23, 2014.

Wu, Jackson. "Authority in a Collectivist Church: Identifying Critical Concerns for a Chinese Ecclesiology." *Contemporary Practice of Global Missiology* 1.9 (October 2011). http://ojs.globalmissiology.org/index.php/english/article/view/679/.

Xi, Lian. *Redeemed by Fire: The Rise of Popular Christianity in Modern China*. New Haven: Yale University Press, 2010.

Xinran. *Buy Me the Sky: The Remarkable Truth of China's One-Child Generation*. Translated by Esther Tyldesley and David Dobson. London: Rider, 2015.

Y. M. Interview with the author, July 8, 2014.

Y. R. Interview with the author, July 9, 2014.

Yao, Rainy. "Golden Years: The Coming Investment Boom in China's Elderly Care Industry." http://www.china-briefing.com/news/2014/09/10/golden-years-coming-investment-boom-chinas-elderly-care-industry.html/.

Ying, Fuk-tsang, Hao Yuan, and Siu-lun Lau. "Striving to Build Civic Communities." *Review of Religion and Chinese Society* 1 (2014) 78–103.

Yuan, Hao. Interview with the author, July 22, 2014.

Yun, Brother, Yongze Xu, Enoch Wang, and Paul Hattaway. *Back to Jerusalem: Three House Church Leaders Share Their Vision to Complete the Great Commission*. Downers Grove, IL: IVP Press, 2005.

Zhang, Shoudong. "The Relationship Between Religious Legislation and Civil Society." http://www.pacilution.com/english/ShowArticle.asp?articleid=3122.

Zhang, Yushuang. "Political Constitution and the Protection of Religious Freedom: A Jurisprudential Reading of Article 36 of the Chinese Constitution." In *Christianity in Chinese Public Life: Religion, Society, and the Rule of Law*, edited by Joel A. Carpenter and Kevin R. den Dulk, 79–96. New York: Palgrave Macmillan, 2014.

Index

Lightning Source UK Ltd.
Milton Keynes UK
UKOW06f1327170316

270320UK00002B/194/P